# Adve~~ntures of a~~
# Londoner who now
# calls Australia home

*Ridiculous, Nostalgic, but
always Enthralling.*

MARY SANGHVI

# CONTENTS

# INTRODUCTION

On 21/11/81 I migrated to Australia from London, with my husband Bharat and our three children, aged as follows: Heidi (8), Jonathan (5) and William (1). These names may pop up now and again in my stories. Usually telling me where I went wrong. Good advice after the event.

This is a collection of mishaps, near disasters, and other ridiculous events. Writing a memoir is a very popular pasttime at the moment, but this isn't exactly a memoir. It highlights some memorable moments in the passage of my seventy-eight years. It is a look at the funny side of life, my life.

I tried to arrange my memories in the order in which they happened, like a memoir. That doesn't always work, because some of the events were too far apart. So I have grouped similar stories. When needed, I have put in a year date. To avoid confusion. Or in case things have changed since then. If you like, you can look at the index and just delve in. You might even be inspired to travel a bit in Australia. Or move here! I have never regretted our move. It is a lovely country to bring up a family and enjoy the great outdoors.

In England, I have written about growing up, crossing on the Channel Ferry to Europe (who does that nowadays?), starting a career, getting myself into trouble with motor cars, living in a boat on the river Thames, and the mayor who made us take down our garden fence, so that he could take his dog for a poo on our lawn. And, of course, our move to Australia.

Then I have taken the trouble to regale you with a bit of Australian history. You are not likely to have learned any of this in school. Which is a pity. At the time of writing, a statue of Captain James Cook has been taken down in Brisbane, in deference to the indigenous people, who are fed up with Australia Day being celebrated as a conquest. Fair enough, they have plenty to complain about, but Captain Cook was not a conquering hero. He bumped into Australia quite by chance, and very accurately charted the whole East Coast, including Botany Bay, where he only went ashore for a few days (while Joseph Banks was collecting botanical specimens). Later, he went aground on the Great Barrier Reef, but miraculously came home to tell the tale and put Australia well and truly on the world map. Somebody was bound to discover Australia sooner or later.

During this story I have touched on world events, and what I thought about them at the time. But this is mostly about Australia. I have now been here forty years, from being a young mother to a granny with seven gorgeous grandchildren.

This is a story of possums and pussy cats; being stuck on the beach in wet bathers on a cold winter morning (because the dog has buried my car keys somewhere in the sand and forgotten about it);  a pine tree falling through our roof; a strange encounter with a sea eagle; an explosion in the pantry and lots more.

I have dreadful battles with technology (despite the fact that I am reasonably tech savvy). The big thing about the twenty-first century is supposed to be communication and the internet.   In reality, it is getting more and more difficult to find a real human being on the other end of a help-line. Maybe there is nobody out there. I have written down my experiences, and I am sure you can relate to them. Apparently, we can communicate with anyone, anywhere in the world, if only we can make the App work.   If we can't master that, we can't catch a taxi,  find the phone (let alone use it), sign on for a well-deserved pension, travel by train, pay our bills, or watch anything interesting on TV.

So these are my stories – enjoy!

# EARLY MEMORIES

## Disappearance

From the very day that we are born, mother nature has given us the gift of self-preservation. We have the instinct of fear and tears. A babe will scream and cry when in need. As we grow up, we are taught to control our behaviour, but little children need their strong emotions to make them scream when in danger. So that Mummy can find them in the woods, before being eaten by a wolf. (I nearly said "dinosaur", but they disappeared sixty million years before mankind walked planet Earth).

My very first memory (when I was about two) is a big sandy beach. Spread in every direction for ever and ever. And I was all alone in the world. Mummy and Daddy were nowhere. So I screamed and cried standing there in my bathers. But then Daddy appeared! He came out of nowhere and he rescued me – this is what I remember.

When you are only very small and your eyes are not very far from your toes, you are looking at the world from a different perspective. Mummy and Daddy may think they are nearby but actually they are over the horizon.

*They have disappeared.*

It all came back to me when babysitting my grandchildren. All is peace and quiet for a few hours, until suddenly mum is wanted.

*I am bored. My big brother is being annoying. Where is Mummy?*

Now my granddaughter Charlie, has just packed her little bag and she's ready to go home.  She is standing at the front door.  Of course Mummy is the other side of the door. Last seen going out through the door. So that's where she is ... but she isn't.

So where is Daddy? Busy in the garden? She's walked around the garden, but he is not there.  Is he in the driveway? No, not there. So this where it gets difficult. This is when the tears come. Because Daddy is no longer in the known world. And that is a terrible thought. Where do Mummy and Daddy go when you can't see them? They go into nowhere. They have vanished forever.

## The Blue Balloon

I had my sixth birthday in Switzerland.  We were there from spring to Autumn. Mummy and I were escaping from smoggy London to the clear mountain air of the Swiss Alps. I had not been well. Repeated attacks of bronchitis kept me away from school. My mother was equally passionately Swiss and English, and spoke Swiss-German fluently, so she asked her family for advice. As a result, she rented the upstairs floor of a farmhouse, in Salisberg, Canton Uri. High above Lake Lucerne. So high, that you can't hear any sound coming up from the lake, and the boats look like match-box toys.

I much prefer the local name for Lake Lucerne. It is called the "Vierwaldstättersee" which is German for the "Lake of the Four Forest Cantons".

Forests, fields, brown cows and goats. The mountains rise straight out of the lake, like the walls of a fairy-tale castle. I remember picking wild blueberries and teen-weeny wild strawberries, in the pine-forest.

I remember the little Swiss flags everywhere, a red square with a white cross inside. The Swiss are very fond of their flag.

I remember the white-and-brown St Bernard dogs, padding along the road, towing their barrel. No, not the famous brandy-barrel round the neck! This was a long, long barrel on wheels, taking the sewage from cess-pits to fertilise the land. Dreadful smell. Hold your nose! But a pretty sight to see.

I remember the folk dancing band that came to the village green. An alphorn (distantly related to a digeridoo), a button accordion, and percussion provided by the dancers themselves. Slapping their hands on their knees and stomping their shoes in the traditional Schuhplattler dance. And, of course, one man dedicated to waving the pretty Swiss flag. Very exciting for a little girl who didn't have much opportunity to hear music.

I remember bath-day in Fraulein Bader's house, where we were staying. Buckets of boiling water were brought in and tipped into the tub. I screamed and jumped out. It's a wonder I wasn't scalded.

I remember holding onto the hem of Mummy's raincoat in a crowded place, and suddenly realising I had the wrong Mummy. Smiles all round.

I remember spending a lot of time looking out of the window, watching the cows in the field below, listening to the mellow sound of their bells. One cow had a bigger, deeper sounding bell. She led the herd into the fields in the mornings and lead them home for milking at the end of the day. And later on, I remember watching the peasants haymaking, with their scythes and their pitch forks.

I remember going to a birthday party for me at my cousin's house in Zurich. To leave Salisberg, we had to descend to Treib, in the funicular railway, and catch a paddle-steamer to Lucerne. We missed the boat. There was a man fishing on the jetty, and Mummy persuaded him to take us in his motorboat. At Lucerne, Auntie Maiti was waiting for us in her beloved Fiat Topolino – "the smallest car in the world" at that time. It was so small, that I had to sit on Mummy's lap. When Auntie had to brake suddenly, I banged my head on the window and bit my tongue. Ouch!

At lunch, an enormous chocolate cake with six candles appeared. I was so surprised, I hid under the table. *"Who told them it was my birthday?"*

I remember watching a puffy white cloud being sucked into the pointy peak of the Fronalpstock, the mountain straight across the lake from us. It was near enough to see the brightly painted huts and the cows in the fields.

Most of all, I remember the blue balloon. I let go of it. We were on the paddle-steamer coming home from Lucerne. I let go of it and it went high into the air.

I screamed, 'Mummy, look! Get it back!"

"I can't. It is a special balloon with gas in it. To make it go up"

" Why didn't you tell me, Mummy?"

Sobbing, I watched my balloon bobbing about in the sky. The sky was blue, the water was blue, and so was my blue balloon. Beautiful, but gone for ever.

*I fell in love with Johanna Spyri's classic novel "Heidi" about a little girl growing up on a mountain, in the Swiss Alps. I could really relate to it. My favourite name was always Heidi. I even named my pet hamster Heidi. My daughter says I named her after a hamster, but that is just not true!*

## Lassies and Laddies

When I was eleven, we went to see Hadrian's Wall, which lies a bit south of the border of Scotland and England. Daddy was a Post Office engineer, and he was testing a new telephone line going from London to Aberdeen. On our journey, everywhere we went, we had to look for a house with no chimney, and for security reasons it looked just like the other bungalows in the street. (This was a Repeater's Station, a kind of telephone exchange, and we would go in and I would wait while he did a lot of technical stuff). But I couldn't help thinking that, if you were a spy, you would know what it was, seeing as all British houses had a fireplace in those days.

Now getting back to Hadrian's Wall. In case you don't know, Hadrian's Wall was ordered by the Roman Emperor in 122 AD, to keep the Scots out. The wall marked the North Western frontier of the Roman Empire. And much of it (eighty miles) is still there. Over the centuries, many of the rocks have been used for building roads and so on. Where we were, it was quite small and I could sit down on it with my feet on the ground, but in some places it is still tall, and some of the garrisons, where the builders and their families lived, are still partly intact.

Incidentally, the first flush toilets to be built in England were in the garrisons on Hadrian's wall. Unfortunately, this concept didn't catch on.

*A recent archaeological dig revealed that the Romans brought their legionaries from far-flung countries such as Syria. And this is where it gets interesting. Apparently, the Roman legionaries could eat anything in a far-off land, provided it was smothered with a fermented fish-sauce, called "garum". This was a traditional Arabic condiment and very popular in the Mediterranean countries. Bottles of the stuff have been found deep-down in the soil, alongside Hadrian's Wall, where the defending soldier's trenches used to be. After two thousand years, the aroma of anchovy lingers on! Garum was manufactured, in very smelly factories at a suitable distance from cities around the Mediterranean Sea. Indeed, it was mass-produced and bottled in amphorae for export. For example, the buried city of Pompei owed its wealth to garum. The favourite ingredient was anchovies. Fishes used, would vary with the seasonal catch.*

I was celebrating my visit to Scotland by wearing a Black Watch tartan skirt. Not a real kilt because those wind round and round. It was a warm, woolly skirt with pleats and looked just like a kilt (traditional men's wear in Scotland).

I was in the public toilets, washing my hands, when an old lady came in and looked at me with annoyance. She said,

"You belong in the laddies, you canna come here," and she had a strong Scottish accent.

So I looked at her and said, "This *is* the Ladies."

"No," she replied sternly, "This is for lassies, and you must go in the laddies."

So I said, "I'm a girl!"

She said, "Then why are you wearing a kilt?"

# My Parents

## Crossing the channel

The English Channel was wide enough to keep out the enemy for 1,000 years. Back in 1066, William the Conqueror invaded England to claim the throne he said was rightfully his. It is said that he burned his boats on the beach to stop his soldiers from jumping into their coracles and rowing back home to Normandy. Fight or else!

Since then, the Channel has kept out Napoleon and Hitler. Before cheap air fares, we were content to be where we were. Europe was across the water and not many people wanted to go there. Much too foreign.

*I remember sitting on the beach with a French friend, Monique, and she said, " Don't you feel trapped on this island?"*

*I looked at her in astonishment.*

*" No, I love the seaside and we have lots of it."*

I was taken aback because we never think of Britain as an island. We have islands: the Isle of White, the Isle of Mann, the Hebrides, the Channel Islands and so on. Even Lindisfarne, the Northumbrian Holy Island with a causeway to the beach at low tide, can be considered an island. Britain is the mainland. Not an island. No, oh no. We're British. Everyone on the other side of the Channel is a foreigner. They are continentals. Europeans who might try to invade. They speak foreign.

Today you can go under the channel in a train tunnel, the "Chunnel". Unsuspecting tourists who have never looked at a map of Europe, don't even know that the Channel is there. They think that England is part of the continent. They get on the train in London, and they get out in Paris or wherever.

Little do they know. Without the channel (I should say the English Channel because we British believe in full possession) the English language would not have spread around the world. The Americans would probably all be speaking Spanish instead of only about half of them. Because it was our windy, damp island, which drove us to sail the Seven Seas.

I have mixed memories of the cross-channel ferry. I remember the excitement of seeing the sea and hearing the gulls and the thrill of starting on a new adventure. And I remember returning home after a long journey, as an adult, and the pleasure of hearing English spoken in the clear voice of the ship's officer on the tannoy speaker.

I remember, when we boarded on a fine day and were looking for a bench with a view, my mother (who had big boobs) asked "Am I going astern?"

"I hope not madam," said the sailor.

That was a bit cheeky. I know she should have said "aft" but Mummy wasn't very good at nautical terms.

Most of all, I remember our summer holidays in Europe. Holidays started with a desperate attempt to get to the ferry on time through narrow country roads. My father speeding like a maniac (keeping up with a sports car on the same mission) in our pre-war Austin 8.

To let you know just how rare it was for British holiday makers to go on a road trip through France, I shall tell you this. I told my teacher that I was going to France with my parents, and she asked me where to. I told her I didn't know. She looked at me pityingly and said, " I expect they will tell you tonight."

If it was a fine day on the Channel, it was lovely sitting on deck and looking at the view. If it was the usual rough weather, the only safe place was the dining room. It was the only place where people weren't throwing up. This was especially true of the French ferries, which dished out enamel bowls to people on deck. On the English ferry, people retired below if they didn't feel well.

The first step, on arriving at Calais or Boulogne, was to remember to drive on the wrong side of the road. Or rather to remember that the right side of the road was the right side of the road. But the usual procedure was to get sworn at in French when leaving the Harbour, by drivers coming in the opposite direction.

At this point, I need to tell you that we were not typical British holiday makers. This was in the days before package tours opened up Benidorm (in sunny Spain) to intrepid British sunshine seekers.

## A wartime love story

My mother met my father, Bill Davis, when she was teaching French and German at the Linguists Club in London, at the beginning of WWII. She had grown up in Switzerland, and he was improving the linguistic ability he had gained when serving in North Africa in the 8th Royal Irish Hussars. He was then working as a telecom engineer with the GPO.

Mummy was most impressed when he turned up for a date in his uniform – he had re-joined the army, this time in the Royal Norfolk's.

The Royal Norfolk's didn't last long. It seems he was a bit late grabbing a motor bike for an exercise and got a dud. And a broken leg. So while his regiment went off to India, Bill hobbled into Westminster Palace to hear Neville Chamberlain declare war on Germany.

After his leg mended, he was transferred to the Royal Signals.  Later, he was seconded to the US army, as a staff officer with General Eisenhower (Ike) in Allied Headquarters in Reims.  I have his original orders, from Ike, in a telegram on paper so thin, that it is almost transparent.

## CONFIDENTIAL

## SUPREME HEADQUARTER ALLIED EXPEDITIONARY FORCE MAIN HEADQUARTERS

**SUBJECT: Orders**

**To  Captain W.B. Davis**

**You will proceed via military aircraft (JOYRIDE) on 4 September1944, from present station to SUPREME HQ AEF in Northwestern France to carry out the instructions of a Chief, Signal Division, SUPREME HQ AEF.**

**Baggage allowance is limited to one hundred (100) pounds.**

While he was with Ike, Bill was responsible for setting up the telecommunications for the Surrender of the German Generals in Reims (and he was present on the occasion). He spent the following two years in command of a small German town, until he was demobbed.  He was awarded the American Medal, but he sent it back on the grounds that he wasn't allowed to accept a gong from a foreign country. Bill was always a stickler about doing the right thing, but some others accepted American medals.

We started taking the car across the channel in the fifties. As soon as Bill was promoted to having three weeks holiday instead of two, we started going on continental holidays to meet the friends and relations. And our first visit was always to an elderly auntie in Monaco, because Mummy worried about her.

Auntie Dora was my Granny's school-friend (at a very Catholic finishing school in Brussels) and my Godmother. She became my Godmother because we went to live with her in Cornwall when I was a baby, as the buzz bombs had started dropping on London. (My Father was away in the army). Later in life, as a widow, Dora married a very charming gentleman who was a native of Monaco. Not a Monegasque, because that honour had to be bought from the Prince of Monaco, and you needed to be a high-roller for that. Uncle was just your ordinary citizen. They were a charming, elderly couple and lived in a tiny flat at the top of a lovely old building. There was definitely no room for visitors to stay.

## The Cote d'Azure

I loved Monaco. From the casino gardens in Monte Carlo, you can look down on an azure sea. Or, at a short walk from the hotel, I could walk down to the harbour, and check out all the fancy yachts at their moorings. The most extravagant, was a white steamer with a yellow funnel, belonging to the Greek magnate Aristotle Onassis, later to be the unlikely husband of President Kennedy's widow, Jacky. I googled it and found that the road to the Port of Monaco is now called John F. Kennedy Boulevard.

We always stayed in the Hotel de Gare, an old-fashioned hotel near Monaco station. I googled again, and it seems to have disappeared. Judging by the flashy international hotels on the web, it would be quite incredibly outdated today. The bedroom windows had a picturesque view of the Rock. The corridor windows, had an intriguing, internal view of our five-storey brick building, which surrounded a square inner-courtyard. At some time in the distant past, bathroom facilities had been tacked on to every suite, like swallows' nests on the walls.

A traditional French birdcage lift, with gilded wrought-iron walls and no roof, took us down to a formal dining room. The lift put my father in mind of his stay in the Hotel de Crillon, in Paris, when he was serving with Ike. His American mates were so impressed with the topless lift, that they started firing their guns at the roof. Daddy called it his most terrifying experience in the whole war.

When the pressure was on, we could we hear the crash of pans and shouting in the kitchen. The waiter told us that we would have to be patient because, "Le chef va piquer une crise!" which can be roughly translated as the chef is having a fit! One evening, a very lively girls' choir from the USA, sent all the waiters quite crazy, and the breakfast service hit an all-time low the following morning.

American tourists could be quite entertaining. We were just amazed to have a shower at all, but a deep American voice next-door, loudly complained, "This shower is so small, I can't turn myself around!"

It was very pleasant to sit on the veranda bistro and have some light refreshment while the world passed by. There is something about a warm Mediterranean evening, which is lacking elsewhere.  We don't have many warm summer evenings (even now that we live in Melbourne).   Or lively French people.

I always longed to live by the sea in a sunny country.  As you can see from this poem I wrote when working in Lancashire, very despondent about work taking up all the daylight hours.

## Life Through a Bus Window

*Written whilst commuting on a Works Bus in an English (Lancashire) winter.*

People
Insignificant people
Standing by the railing
Standing by the trees.

Drab,
Dressed for dull skies
Muffled and subdued...
Waiting for buses.

Windows

With the rain

Perpetual rain

Running down the panes

Trickling in dirty droplets

Transparent barrier to the world.

Life

Life from a bus window

Seen

But untouchable

Uncontrollable

Inevitable.

Glimpsed between night and day

Between darkness, and captivity.

We are but cogs

Caught in the complicated

Machinery

Of the era of technology.

# MOTORING MISHAPS

## What a disappointment!

My father inspected the car I had bought.

*He said, "Where was that dug up?"*

*I said, "No need to be rude,"*

*He said, "I am not being rude. I seriously think it was buried and dug up."*

I bought my first car in Lancashire, when I was learning to drive. It was bright blue, an old Ford Anglia. One of those models that looked much the same at both ends. Needless to say, it was going for a song at some shonky dealer. But who cares as long as it starts with a few pulls on the choke, and fairly reliably gets to its destination.

At the time, I was an undergraduate, doing a six-month slot with the UK Atomic Energy Authority in Culcheth. I travelled from the hostel to work, with an intrepid Welsh student who didn't mind supervising me in exchange for a lift. I was trying to do my mirror-checking thing, to the extent that I was looking more behind than ahead. He gave me a piece of good driving advice that I have never forgotten. Here it is (if you'll excuse the Celtic tongue):

*"Bugger the man behind". After all, if someone runs into the back of your car, it is generally considered to be their fault.*

Culcheth is a village in the County of Warrington, and I was taking driving lessons in the city of Warrington.    There was a reasonable road through open countryside (in fact you could get up a good speed) between Culcheth and Warrington.  But there is just one bend (almost a hairpin bend) on the way.

Now the windscreen wipers on the car, were powered in a way that I believe to be unique.  There was a metal cylinder, about a foot long and 3 inches wide. It used pressure from somewhere or the other, to drive the wipers. Unfortunately, it had a leak. I was to discover that, on driving to Warrington on a rainy day.   The road was straight with a wide view of farmland in all directions.  For some unknown reason (most probably a property boundary) there was a sharp bend in the middle of nowhere.  As soon as I braked, preparatory to going round the bend, both windscreen wipers speeded up, crossed over each other, and fell off.  I had to stop the car, find the wipers and fix them on again.  It turned out, that this always happened, at that spot.

When I returned home to London, my father reconditioned the wiper thing, commenting that it was  covered in rust and mud and had definitely been buried.  I was inclined to put its state down to the consistently wet and windy climate in Lancashire.

Needless to say, I took my driving test in the instructor's car. It was a memorable experience. One feature was an emergency stop. The examiner had a clacker, to simulate an emergency. I was worried that I had not reacted well enough.

Then we went through an area of assisted housing and there were kids playing in the street. A little boy ran onto the road, right in front of us. I slammed on the brakes. The examiner was in a bit of shock and so was I. When the test was finished, he said,

"Thanks to that grubby urchin, you have definitely passed the test. And thank you for reacting so fast."

When I was back at university, the time came up for my car to have its MOT road safety test. It failed. In those days, Brunel University was housed in a long four-story building off the Uxbridge Road, in Acton. I had parked next to the wire fencing on the driveway, and I was just telling a friend about the MOT, when we saw a large delivery truck, driverless, travelling downhill from the service entrance, toward my car. Then it veered and smashed into the fence instead. I was so relieved; I had really thought my car was a goner. But my friend was quick to see I had missed out. He said:

"What a disappointment! That would have solved your MOT problem."

## Madam can't open her mouth

*A journalist friend wanted to throw a party for Prince Charles in our share house, in which I lived with four other girls. We said "Yes" but did not really expect that his Royal Highness would be allowed to come. He had just begun as a fresher, at Cambridge University.*

My housemates included three state-registered-nurses, two of which were called Liz, and were dubbed Wee Liz and Big Liz – to avoid confusion.

On the day of the party, I am driving home on the A10 when I start to feel very drowsy. I do make it to the house, and I'm given the task of making sandwiches. The odd thing is, I can't cut the bread. I seem to have lost my concentration. I just can't do it. So I set out a loaf, some cheese and a breadknife on a platter. It seems very strange that I can think out a solution but can't cut the bread.

It so happens that I am going out to dinner before the party. A family friend from Germany, who is staying with my parents, is coming up to Cambridge for the day, and we arranged to meet. Henning picks me up in his car and we go to a very posh Chinese restaurant.

We order the meal, but when the chicken-and-corn soup arrives, I have a problem.  My jaw starts cramping, and I can't get the soupspoon into my mouth.

We cancel the meal.

The waiter fetches the head waiter – What is wrong?  Don't we like the soup?

"The soup is fine," says Henning, "but Madam cannot open her mouth."

We stop at my doctor's house on the way home – he asks if I suffer from asthma.  I say yes.  He says, " Then it could be the pills that I prescribed you for your tummy trouble."

We get home and I am feeling worse. My housemates work at Addenbrookes hospital.  Wee Liz thinks I might have lockjaw (tetanus).  She nursed a little boy with it, and he recovered. Wee Liz, Henning and I go to the hospital.  Have I got any cuts? No. Take all your clothes off. Wee Liz suspects they are perving. One of them is engaged to a housemate. Wee Liz won't let him look.

No cuts.

They give me some sedation to stop my jaw seizures.  Next morning, I wake up in a ward. Someone is selling newspapers and magazines. I want to buy a magazine, but I haven't got a purse with me.   The lady in the bed opposite kindly buys one for me.  Problem!  I can't read it. The print is clear, but the words mean nothing to me.

The hospital keeps me under observation for a couple of days.  I can now eat, but I still can't read.   While I am in hospital, I see the psychiatrist in case it is psychosomatic.

He is questioning me on whether I have ever done anything irresponsible.  The only thing I can think of is this story.

*My car is an old Ford Anglia.   One of the ones with the distinctive slope back rear window.  It is unreliable starting. I usually depend on the damsel-in-distress reaction of some young man passing by, to give my car a push.  Unfortunately, in this instance, there are no passers-by. I am in Kent Gardens in West Ealing.  It is quite a steep hill, and I am near the top of it.  If I put it in gear and just get out a moment and give a little push, it might start up the engine.    But no!  When I give it a little push, it starts moving fast, in fact it disappears down the hill.  This is very worrying, because at the bottom of the hill, Kent Gardens intersects with Pitshanger Lane, which is a bus-route with shops.*

*I have visions of my car, smashed by a bus.   Or in some other nasty accident, possibly involving an injured child or a mother pushing a pram.  But when I arrive at the intersection, there is still no sign of it.  In fact, my car has successfully crossed the road, without incident.   This is the bottom of the hill. And there is my car, neatly parked in front of the wrought iron gates of Pitshanger Park.  It slowed to a halt just in time.  And hooray! The engine is running.*

The psychiatrist takes this story very seriously.  It seems that what I thought was an error of judgement, was an indication that I was suffering from a state of mind known as "Happy go lucky".

When I was discharged, the Matron wanted a word with me.   I was dressed and ready to go, and she was standing with her back against the door.   What she had to tell me was that the psychiatrist was offering to give me a course of treatment. That was a message from him.

"You are definitely not obliged to make an appointment with a psychiatrist," she said quietly, "the doctor says that your problem was an extra-pyramidal reaction to the medication you were taking.  Nothing psychosomatic."

I was keen to know whether Prince Charles had come to the party.  Apparently not.  In fact, none of us, the hostesses, were there.   Rosemary had gone to buy booze but got distracted and went somewhere else.   Wee Liz was with me at the hospital.  I am not quite sure what happened to the other two.

**Postscript:**   It took three weeks for the extra-pyramidal effects to wear off. This was a worry, because I was studying for my university final examinations, and I couldn't read. Fortunately, I was better in time for the actual exams. My symptoms were caused by medication. I had been prescribed oestrogen tablets, to change my menstrual cycle.  My periods were very regular, and terribly painful, and so it was highly likely that I would miss at least one exam. A bit unfair after four years of study. The idea was to alter my cycle by making me a week late, the month before. Unfortunately, this gave me morning sickness – hence my visit to the local GP for something to calm my tummy. I think he was a bit out of his depth, because he prescribed me a tranquilizer (trifluoperazine hydrochloride) which is nowadays only prescribed as an anti-psychotic medication.

## The garage disaster

I have a distant memory of going to a Careers Show with my school, and being very impressed by a display on technical journalism. I've always enjoyed writing and was good at it. But I didn't think I was ready to write a novel, as I had no real experience of life. So scientific journalism seemed a very good option, and I must have kept it in the back of my mind, because after I graduated with an Honours degree in Applied Physics, I applied for an editorial position at International Business Press (publishers of The Daily Mirror and The New Scientist). In fact, the very same company that had caught my eye at the show. I was editing a journal called "Non-destructive Testing". Not a very inspirational title.

*I had already had enough of working in scientific research. My university course was a "sandwich course" at Brunel University, involving spending 6 months of the year in industry. My industrial sponsor was the United Kingdom Atomic Energy Authority (UKAEA) at Harwell. I was working in cyclotron group. I never saw the cyclotron as it was underground.  It was only run occasionally. Then our guys would crawl around on hands and knees checking if all the cables were plugged in and some Oxford University scientists would turn up and do their experiments.*

*A cyclotron is a machine which shoots particles down a very long tube, shaped like a Catherine wheel. It's like shooting a microscopic bullet at a target, except that this bullet is accelerating all the way.*

*Why this is done is beside the point.  My point is, that while the experiment was running, scientists would be staring at monitor screens, and getting excited about it.   I think I can tell you, without being punished (exterminated?) for breaking the Official Secrets Act, that the thing that was exciting them was a new kink in a kinky line on the screen:*

*"Have we seen that before?  Is it new? Can I put my name on it?"*

*Well, really!*

*I decided that there was absolutely no way that my claim to fame would be a squiggle.  Scientific research was not for me. However, I must say that life at Harwell was a lot of fun, and I made very good friends there.*

Getting back to the subject, the editorial office was in Guildford, Surrey.  So I needed to find accommodation.  I started off by boarding (with breakfast and dinner) in a private house, with a view to house-sharing later. I actually only lasted a week. This is how it happened.

I was allowed to use the garage behind the house, because Mr Jones was on an overseas assignment. The garage was behind the kitchen. There was a little driveway beside the house, but not enough room for a garage so you had to do a quick right-and-left to drive in. But that was not my undoing. Disaster happened when I tried to get out in the morning.

The garage was entirely built of timber, and had two doors which latched in the middle. It was not an up-and-over. I had just put my car into reverse, when I noticed in my mirror, that the garage door on my right was swinging shut. So I opened my door to jump out and fix it, forgetting that taking my foot off the clutch would set the car in motion. Before I could even properly get out, my door caught the garage door.

This had the amazing effect of removing the entire right-hand wall of the garage.

Fortunately, my car was not badly damaged as it had slowed down by the time it hit the kitchen wall. I braked in time for that. But the garage was a heap of planks.

Mrs Jones asked me to do something about it before Mr Jones came home on Friday. I phoned my friend Graham, who lived in hall at Brunel. By an amazing coincidence, he was just passing the phone booth, and promised to come straightaway.

Graham was fully sponsored by IBM and always wore a suit. I can still picture him now, standing there, gaping at my morning's work.

"I thought you were exaggerating. I bought a hammer and nails on my way down."

We tried to find a builder to fix it before Friday, but without success.

Mrs Jones said, "Could you please organise to move out before Friday. I think it would be wise."

## The Measles

I did manage to find lodgings, before Friday. I cannot remember how or where I cooked, but I do remember that on my corridor, there was another bedroom and a rather creepy bathroom. Beryl had the other bedroom, and we became good friends. We decided to look for a flat to share, but that took a while to find.

The lodgings was about a kilometre up the road from my office. I was half-way home, when I felt as if all my energy had suddenly been sucked out of me. It was that sudden, as if I had been knocked on the head. I had to struggle to walk. When I got there, I knocked on the door and told my landlady that I was feeling really ill, with a high fever.

"Oh, you must have measles," she said, "My little boy has it."

I missed out on catching the measles as a child, because I didn't start school until I was eight and I was puzzled because I had no contact with the little boy. But I remembered that I put my head in the door to ask for telephone messages. In the light of what we now know about viruses, I could have caught it from the kitchen doorknob.

It was a rather strange evening. A young insurance salesman came round to renew my car insurance. I was in bed feeling awful, and I told him that I probably had measles. He went down on his knees and tried to sell me a life-insurance. I managed to get rid of him. Then an Irish boyfriend dropped by. That was nice. He wasn't worried about the measles.

When my father picked me up to go home, his carriage wasn't in line with the platform when the train stopped at the station. So he pulled the emergency cord. He did not get fined. He drove me home in my car. I got quite sick, with a fever, a really bad cough, and a rash that tingled as if something was crawling under my skin. I was off work for nearly three weeks.

When I went back, they were surprised to see me. My boss thought I had walked out on them. Their admin had sent me a form, which I had filled out and sent to the address given. But that was the address of the head-office in London, and no-one had sent it on. So I had already been replaced. No matter, I was given a journal called Ultrasonics to edit. This was quite interesting, and I even reported on a medical conference at the University of Lyons in France. That was amazing. Imagine a hologram of a beating heart, looking rather like a ghost in Harry Potter!

Beryl and I found a flat opposite the rowing-club on the River Wey, just a few minutes' walk from my office. It was a lovely spot to be in.

# MYSTIC CONNECTIONS

## Holiday in Viareggio

On the spur of the moment, while I was at University, I decided to go for a two-week holiday and Italian course, which happened to be in Viareggio, a holiday town in Tuscany.  I have a certificate for it from the University of Pisa. This represents my only formal education in the Italian language!  Just now I am refreshing it at the U3A.   I met my room-mates, Val and June in Victoria station. They were sitting on their suitcases with the rest of the party. The three of us had answered a last-minute advert in the Evening Standard. We had never met before. We were to share a room in a family house, while everyone else lived in the school.

We all three slept in the same bedroom. During the day, it was safe to open the windows, but we had to remember to shut them in time to keep out the mosquitoes.  I remember being woken up by Val sitting up in her sleep screaming, "A mosquito smashed the window. And it's going to bite me!"

Val had just completed her first year of Italian at Leeds University, and she remarked, "How come you can talk Italian with your eyes shut, when they knock on the door to wake us up!" I had picked up a bit of the language from going to Italy on road-trips with my parents. (Quite an unknown holiday activity at that time but my mother loved Italy and my father was game for anything).

The holiday was the source of remarkable coincidences, involving Val, June, a Turkish girl called Zeren, and Claire Jennings, whom I was to meet in my first journalism job:

(a) I had not yet met Bharat, but six years later, soon after we were married, we went to lunch with Val's parents at their home, and Val's father said, "I know you. Aren't you Rajnikant Sanghvi's son? I was you father's bank manager in East Africa." In fact they had regular business meetings and were well acquainted.

(b) I was about to take up 6-months' work experience at the Atomic Energy Authority in Culcheth, Lancashire – very close to June's home, so it was good to make a friend in the locality.

(c) I had not yet met Claire but Claire's Aunt lived next-door to June's parents in Lancashire. Later on when I was in my first journalism job, Claire was our office secretary and we became very good friends and she became my son William's Godmother Furthermore, when I was nineteen, I had stayed with a family in Turkey, to give English conversation, and my mother and I had arranged for Zeren to go to a Finishing

School in Sussex.

Would you believe, Claire was her room-mate!

To sum up:

**Claire and Zeren:** I had not met Claire yet, but at this time she was room-mates with Zeren, in finishing school. I knew Zeren because friends of her family had a son staying at our house (the friends now lived in Germany), and they asked if I would like to have a holiday in Turkey, and be Zeren's English-speaking companion. So when I was nineteen, I had a very memorable holiday with them, on the island of Buyuk Ada, in the sea of Marmara.

**June:** June lived in the village of Culcheth, in Lancashire, where I was going to be working when I came home from Viareggio. Claire's Aunt lived next-door to June's parents.

**Val:** Val's father knew my future husband's family well, when they lived in Tanzania, and recognised Bharat immediately, when we visited her parents, ten years later.

There was absolutely no connecting link between June and Val.

It all sounds like one of those logic puzzles in the Better Homes and Gardens Puzzle Book. But there is nothing logical about it.

Is it all a remarkable coincidence – or does Viareggio have some mystic significance? My mother spent happy holidays there, in her youth.

Maybe, the connection was simply that all three of us (me, June and Val) were ready and willing to go off to Italy on the spur of the moment! All three of us, had a two-week break that needed filling.

But that doesn't account for Val's family knowing my future husband! I certainly had absolutely no idea, that I would one-day be marrying an Indian from Tanzania.

# MARRIAGE

## Look after Mary

It wasn't so bad being an only child, because our house was interestingly filled with students from the Kensington School of Languages. They had come to London to learn English, and live in an English family.

It all started when my cousin Otto came to stay. He was sixteen and I was seven. My mother loved his visit (she was a bit homesick for Switzerland) and she said, "Why don't we buy a bigger house and have some students *en famille* (as paying guests)?" So we did. And this went on until my father retired.

We were under strict instructions (from the agency) to always speak English, unless there was an emergency. My mother spoke several languages; including French, Italian, German and Swiss German, all of which she spoke fluently. My father could speak French and German. In fact, they met when she was teaching in Night School at the Linguist's Club. He was in her class.

Hospitality is a two-way thing. I got to know people from all over the world. All sorts of people. Some stayed for a few weeks, some stayed for a year. Here are a few of the memorable ones:

There was the French teenager from Senegal who took another guest shoplifting in the West End. This was the only embarrassing experience my mother ever had with the guests. The girls had to appear in Old Street Court-house (as in Monopoly) with a long line of local prostitutes, paying their regular fines. The girl from Senegal was happily dancing Chubby Checker's "Twist, Twist and Twist Again" in her cell, while her Greek companion was absolutely stricken and ashamed. She had come to London to have her nose remodelled, so that she could find a suitable husband. I couldn't see anything wrong with her nose, and she had a sweet personality. Clearly, being arrested for shoplifting was not a part of her improvement program and, even more scary, one of her friends died under anaesthetic having the same operation.

There was a Finnish businessman who reported that he had travelled to England via a Russian ship which had thirteen accommodation classes. There are thirteen ways of serving our bortsch! An interesting insight into communism.

And there was a German university student who was helping refugees to escape from East Germany, across the Berlin wall. His father visited us too. The father had spent months walking home from Russia at the end of the WWII. Lucky to have survived any of that.

Because I was used to having foreigners living in the family, and because I enjoyed speaking French, when I heard that there was a local International Club in Guildford, I decided to try it out. It was actually run at the local church, which had a hall big enough for dancing and a table-tennis room. The "internationals" in Guildford turned out to be "au pair" girls, working as nannies, and boys from Commonwealth countries, studying at the university.

I was greeted by two grey-haired aunties, who introduced me to Bharat and his friend Parry, with the instruction, "Look after Mary".

Bharat was an Indian from East Africa, and his friend Parry was a Pakistani Londoner. Bharat is quite fair-skinned for an Indian (his family was from the state of Gujerat in Northwest India), and when I asked him where he was from, I thought he said "Bangkok". There isn't a long-O sound in the Gujarati language, and he was trying to say, "Burnt Oak," which is where he was living in London.

*That was a fortunate misunderstanding. Had I known Bharat was Indian, I would probably have run a mile. Coming from Ealing, which includes the "Turban" district of Southall, I had a bad impression. The local rubber factory was bringing in cheap labour from villages in the Punjab. I doubt that their employers gave guidance on how to behave in a foreign land. They certainly did not warn them not to bother girls in the street. Our local paper ran some interesting stories:*

*Two rubber workers appeared in the Magistrates Court, because they took it into their heads to kidnap a girl on the London Underground. It seems they didn't think further ahead than the kidnapping. So she was frightened but unharmed.*

*The workers were also given to brewing their own hooch, and driving on fake licenses. The licences were fairly convincing, except that all had the same typo – "Gondon" instead of London. The result was drunken moped driving and some unfortunate accidents involving pedestrians.*

Getting back to "Look after Mary", there was music and dancing in the hall that evening, and the three of us sat down together, watching the dancing. Bharat asked me to dance, and although he was rather lovely, I said,

"No, but I will tell you who to dance with."

He was a bit taken aback, but I pointed someone out and he went and asked her, and they danced. Then he came back and said, "Who next?" We carried on with that, and I occasionally danced with Parry.

Then Bharat mentioned that there was going to be a dance at the Uni. I said I would bring my flatmate, Beryl. I actually didn't realise he was asking me as his date!

Beryl and I decided to walk to the dance. That turned out to be much harder than expected, because the University of

Surrey (formerly Battersea Tech) was still largely a building site. We were picking our way through the bricks and pavers, singing "We are off to see the Wizard, the Wonderful Wizard of Oz," to cheer us on our way. It made us think of the Yellow Brick Road because some of the pavers were yellow.

We bumped into some boys I knew and went into the dance with them. But I had to go downstairs to phone my dad to say that I wasn't coming home for the weekend. I was just going back up the stairs, when Bharat called out, "Sorry we are late!" He had brought his (English) friend Ray, with him for Beryl.

And funnily enough we all paired up. I married Bharat, Ray married Beryl, and Parry married Leah (a Dutch au pair he met at the International Club). We went to their wedding in Holland. This all took a few years to eventuate.

And it is my belief that all this happened because of the words, "Look after Mary." Those were the magic words that went into his subconscious mind! In my husband's culture, every man expects to have his wife picked out for him by his Mum, an auntie or his elder brother's wife.

## Starry, starry night – Living in a boat on the Thames

I had a one-year contract as an encyclopaedia writer for a publisher in Russell Square. (Grolier Inc was outsourcing to the UK). At that time Bharat and I were living on the river Thames, on a mooring in Twickenham. We were on the tidal side of Twickenham weir. To get to our boat, we first had to go down a long gangplank from the boatyard to a barge called the "John and Mary". The plank was very steep at low tide.

After the "John and Mary" we had to put a leg over the rail to get on to the next boat, which was also quite a large one, then climb into a smallish boat (lower on the water). The final step was to jump down into our boat, which was a Norfolk Broads cruiser and pretty much in the middle of the river.

Our boat was a Norfolk Broads hire cruiser, which we bought for five hundred pounds. All boats in the fleet were named after Knights of the Round Table, and ours was Sir Galahad. We renamed it Starry Night (without a K) after the song by Don McLean, which was rising in the charts at the time.

Starry Night was our first married home. By coincidence, the same week I took on a new job as a writer. This meant commuting to Russell Square, by catching the train from Strawberry Hill to Waterloo, where I went down the escalator to catch the tube to Old Street. It was a one-year contract, and the funny thing was that the cinema near the station was showing the same movie all that year - it was called "Danish dentist on the job". I never actually saw people going in or out of the cinema so I can't tell you who watched it.

Living in the middle of the river Thames had its moments.  A white tom-cat decided to adopt us. As a token of his affection and undying love, he decided to bring us a live mouse at six o'clock in the morning.  Then he did the cat trick of stirring it up before killing it, the two of them jumping all over the bunk.  It was not a nice experience, and we decided to ban him after that.

Bumping about on the river could come in handy.   I can't remember why we had let an insurance salesman come on board, but we couldn't get rid of him. I decided to get ready for bed, and I went in the galley to clean my teeth. Turning on the tap activated a rather noisy water pump.  At the same time, a yacht passed by (raising a lot of wash), making our boat rock wildly.

*"What's all the noise?"  asked Mr Insistent Salesman.*

*"It's just the pump"*

*"Are we going to sink?"*

He was off the boat in seconds.

The boat was twenty-eight feet long and nine feet in the beam i.e. it was less than 3 metres at the widest point. Our bed was in the cabin at the pointy end, and there was a dinette in the main cabin. The cockpit was aft of our bedroom. There was a small galley with two hot-plates in the stern, and I cooked most meals in my pressure cooker. We had a chemical toilet, which was regulation on the river. We had to be very economic with water, as the sink taps worked on an electric pump driven by the same battery that started the engine. Plus we had to fill up the water tank. The boat-engine was a diesel, and the smell of diesel still makes me feel nostalgic for the river.

Being at the pointy end, we had to have a pointy mattress. I measured the bunk up carefully and bought a rectangular foam rubber mattress, cut to shape. Then I bought a big strip of waterproof, navy vinyl, cut it to fit the mattress and sewed it up on my sewing-machine. What a challenge! Just as well it was waterproof, as it turned out the deck had a bit of a of a leak. Until we fixed it, with a few layers of paint, we wore beanies in bed, in case of rain.

On Starry Night, we had to make sure that the fenders were in order – plus other nautical odds-and-ends. I had a rather embarrassing experience in a boat-yard:

*I'm reversing my car into a parking-spot and I can't twist and look over my shoulder, because I am heavily pregnant. I'm not familiar with the car park, and I've never been very good at reversing. There is an ominous BUMP and a CLUNK and the car comes to a sudden halt. I get out, and to my horror, the rear wheels are in mid-air, hanging over the edge of a wall. Oh my God, is it going to tip over, and land in the river? It's one of those seesawing, movie cliff-hanger moments! I look down, and to my relief, it is not over water. The back of my car is about a metre above the towpath.*

Picture me, looking very pregnant, wearing a loose, pink, hippy kaftan standing beside my car in some dismay.

Fortunately, the River Police Patrol boat was passing by, and I waved to them frantically.  Four burly policemen immediately landed, and easily lifted my car on to terra firma. I thanked them profusely.  They just grinned, and said OK.

At low tide, the gang-plank to the John and Mary, was very steep.  After I narrowly survived  a perilous descent (carrying a whole water melon) we decided to  look for a better mooring, for the sake of our unborn child.  We were very lucky to find a mooring with its own little garden, at Tagg's Island, near Hampton Court Palace.

Our next-door neighbour, owning a big lump of the island, was Jimmy Nervo (who achieved fame as a comedian in the Crazy Gang, during World War II).  I went next-door to borrow some sugar, in an unexpected heat-wave, wearing only my bathers.  Being heavily pregnant, I got a bit of banter from Jimmy, as you can imagine.  He had a young visitor with him, Mark Lester, who was quite marvellous as Oliver in the 1968 movie Oliver Twist (when he was only 8 years old). I recognised him immediately, from his curly blond hair and pretty face. He lived with his parents in a baby-blue, two-story flat-afloat, moored on the opposite bank.

Just now, I googled Mark on Wiki, and found that he was a big star throughout his childhood but more or less retired from that, when his accumulated earnings became accessible to him on his eighteenth birthday. Then he allegedly (according to Wiki) went a bit wild for a while, took his A-levels when he was 28 and became an osteopath specialising in sports injuries!

Would you believe (according to Wiki) Mark Lester was godfather to three of Michael Jackson's children, and in 2013, claimed to be the biological father of Paris Jackson. Lester claimed that he was one of twenty sperm-donors involved with fathering Jackson's children, and offered to take a paternity test. Showbiz is a strange world!

Our other next-door neighbour, Arthur, was piano-man in a backing band. His wife was a nurse, and she was pregnant too. Sadly, they lost the baby because he was born with no duodenum. Consequently, he couldn't nourish. The doctors tried to save him, but he was tiny and did not survive the operation. The doctors said that this fault may have been genetically passed on, due to Arthur having had a duodenal ulcer which had nearly killed him. I remember that Arthur played the piano all night, in his grief, and he played most beautifully. I am very glad to say that their next baby was absolutely fine.

According to a recent documentary, Tagg's island is now a bit of a haven for old rockers! Back in the day (in 1872, to be precise) Thomas Tagg built the Thames Hotel on the island, which attracted High Society and even Royalty. It went a bit downhill after World War 1, and is now owned by the houseboat residents, like us. Except, that we were renting the land, when we were there. The owner of our little plot, came round monthly to collect the rent. I remember him well,  in his flashy sportscar,  complaining that he "didn't have two pennies to rub together".

The boat was fun, but it was a lot like camping. We enjoyed tootling upriver at the weekends and mooring up at Magna Carta Island, or Henley or Windsor.  However, when the baby was due, we sold it and rented a ground floor flat with a nice garden, in Acton.

# The Fence

1980

Before migrating to Australia, we were living in Hoddesdon, in the Hundred Acre Estate. In Australia, you wouldn't get many houses into a hundred acres, but this was England and there were streets and streets of them. The design was quite ingenious. Every cul-de-sac opened on to a circular road which had no houses. It was the connecting link. In the middle, there was a primary school and a small shopping parade. All the kids could walk to school without having to worry about crossing a road. Kids from the outer side of the ring road, crossed by an underpass in front of the school.

Our back-garden was the smallest in the row of four houses at the bottom of the close. Each garden after that was progressively longer. Half our lawn was taken up by a Hill's hoist. We were the end house and then there was a fence ending in a row of four garages. That fence and our side-fence, formed the short sides of a triangular patch of grass, which was totally unused. We had the bright idea of extending the garden, so that the kids would have plenty of room to play. Our house backed on to the ring-road and this bit of land opened on to the ring road. This necessitated building a fence. The idea was to move our side-fence and add a bit more fencing.

My job was to get the thing organised and my husband's job was to move the fence. I went down to the town hall to find out if we could. The town planner told me there was a problem, the land didn't belong to the council. So who did it belong to? Unfortunately, it belonged to the Highways. He could, however, give me a permit to cultivate.  In other words, for a peppercorn rent, we could grow flowers on the verge in front of our garden.  I said I didn't want to grow flowers; I wanted my children to play safely. So, he suggested that we ask our neighbours if they would have any objection.  If they didn't, we could put up a fence at our own risk.

The next step was to chat to our neighbours.  I knew them all well, it was a friendly environment. All our kids played together.  In fact, the neighbours were delighted at the idea. The local teenagers had recently discovered that they could take a short-cut into town in the evenings, by going down our street and prising a few planks off the fence joining our house to the garage block.  There seemed to be no stopping them!  Furthermore, the grass was full of dog poo.

I took out the Licence to Cultivate, and my husband started on the project.  It was a learning curve, and the hardest bit was removing the fence posts in the side fence.  But all went well, Bharat got the hang of nailing boards into place and within a few days of very hard work, the job was finished.

Now this is when the trouble started. We had not thought to ask the people on the other side of the ring-road.  In fact, there was only one house actually facing across the road to our new bit of garden.   Unfortunately, it was inhabited by a former Mayor.  He was very indignant, and he demanded that we take it down immediately.  Apparently, he took his dog there every morning, for a poo. As soon as the job was complete, he put in a complaint, accusing us of stealing the land.

I thought it pretty nasty that he waited until the job was finished before saying anything. Surely, he could have spoken to us when we first started. He was threatening to send people in to tear down the fence immediately, and take it away. He didn't speak to us at all, I never saw him face-to-face. I sent a reply saying that my children would be put at risk until we could buy a new fence, and I would inform the press.

"It will make a good news story, with me holding my baby with my little children beside me, standing in my garden while you tear down the fence on to the street."

We had a short reprieve, long enough to do the job again in reverse. My neighbours were quite disappointed about the whole thing.

A year later, when I told my next-door neighbour, Judy, that we were migrating to Australia, her reaction was,

"I don't blame you. That fence business was enough to make anybody go to Australia."

# Leaving England

November 1981

There are three removal men in my sitting-room, drinking cups of tea. They don't show any sign of removing anything. In fact, they turned up with a van that was already almost full. This is a bit of a worry, as we are moving out tonight, and flying to Australia in two days' time.

I have spent the last few weeks going through all our stuff, room by room. I have three heaps: ship: plane; and get rid of it. My rule is: anything that costs more to ship than to replace in Australia, should stay behind. Shipping is charged by volume, so size is important. We are not sending the car, the beds, or anything tatty, onto the ship. Also, the ship is going to take three months to arrive, so with three kids to entertain, a suitcase of toys and games is going on the plane. (This was a fortunate decision. In 1981, toys were expensive and not abundant, in Australia.)

My cleaning lady has come in to help with the move, and she is making cups of tea. At last, an empty removal van arrives, driven by the foreman. The tea-drinkers all get back in their van and disappear! Leaving the foreman to pack and load a houseful, by himself.

Bharat has gone to my dad's house to pick up a few of my things, and is well overdue. I don't know what's going on. Remember, we are talking about life before the mobile phone. It's getting dark, and beginning to snow. We are all a bit fuddled with a fluey cold. Bharat and Daddy made a poor decision. They decided they were running a bit late, and would take a shortcut through London, instead of taking the North Circular Road. Bad move! It took five hours to cross from Ealing to Hoddesdon. The traffic was terrible in the city.

Bharat is bringing Daddy, because we are going to drop off the car to its new owner, and we will need a lift to London. To make things even more complicated, Daddy has the Annual Regimental Reunion dinner to go to. There aren't many officers still alive and kicking, so he needs to go.

To make things worse, we are all a bit fuddled with the flu, and hardly know what we are doing. It's getting dark and snow is falling. By the time they arrive, darkness has fallen, and the removal van has gone. The purchaser of our car, who has so kindly agreed to let us keep it until today, lives in Harlow, Essex. About half-an-hour away. We set off with me and baby William in our car with Bharat, Heidi and Jonathan in the car with Grandad.

I am navigating (no GPS in 1981) and I have a piece of paper with the purchaser's directions on it. We miss the turn on a major roundabout, and have to go round again. We've lost Grandad! I get out of the car and stand on the lookout to wave him down if he comes past – but all I can see is headlights. What with the darkness and the falling snow, visibility is nil. I get back in the car and we continue, and then I realise that the address isn't on my bit of paper. I must have noted it somewhere else. We are looking at a block of flats. Oh, calamity!

Fortunately, they were looking out for us (and their new car) and came down. We go upstairs and complete the transaction, and phone Bharat's cousin Satish, who lives in Tottenham (famous for the Tottenham Hotspurs soccer team). Then they kindly drop us at the station. Remember that Heidi and Jon are with Grandad, who wants to go to his reunion, but that isn't going to happen, because we are not there.

We are waiting in Tottenham underground station, standing holding William's hands. He is a sweet little boy, and he's wearing a fluffy white hoody. He is one-and-a-half. An icy-cold wind is blowing down the stairs, to the hall where we are standing. By coincidence, Tottenham is the station where Bharat changes trains every day. He is not happy. He thought he had seen the last of it! Am I glad when Satish picks us up and takes us home to dinner.

All family members rallied round us that weekend. Bharat dropped the extra furniture at the removalists. He caught one of them playing his guitar. The packing hadn't been done yet. We stayed at Bharat's uncle's for the week-end, and various family members transported us to the airport. The whole performance cured me of the wish to move house ever again. I have friends who move often but, forty years later, I am still happily living in the house we bought on arrival in Australia.

When I told friends and neighbours that we were migrating to Australia, they said, "How brave!" I have never regretted moving here. We flew at our own expense, and were very surprised to be signed on to unemployment benefit at the airport, in Melbourne. We had sold our house, and were well-qualified. We already had friends and family here.

We chose Melbourne because Bharat's younger brother Dipak was already settled here, with a young family and his own pharmacy. And a wide circle of friends. Eventually, Bharat's parents and his other two brothers migrated to Australia. Now, forty years later, there is a whole clan of us! And we are no longer the only mixed marriage.

On the advice of friends, when we came to Australia, we decided to settle in Melbourne's Eastern suburbs in the city of Frankston, gateway to the beautiful Mornington Peninsula. House prices were very reasonable, and I have always loved the seaside. A five-minute drive takes us into rural Victoria, or to a sandy beach in Port Philip Bay. Melbourne stands at the North of the bay, with suburban spread down the East and West coasts. A century ago, there were marshes between Frankston and the inner suburbs. So it is a very self-sufficient town. No need to go elsewhere, unless for a special event. Good schools, shopping, restaurants, wineries, beaches, sports clubs for the kids ... I still love it here. And it is commutable to Melbourne, being at the end of the metropolitan train service.

We were able to find a five-bedroom house with a granny flat for my father, for less than a small three-bedroom house would have cost us in the inner suburbs.   It stands on a one-third-of-an-acre block, which at that time had no flowerbeds – only a small forest!    A park (with football, cricket and tennis facilities) across the road, a primary school within walking distance – a great place to bring up a family.

I now realise that settling down in Australia was a very different thing for the migrants who had come as ten-pound poms on a sea-passage. Last night, I saw the "Working Class Man" biopic of the iconic Australian singer, Jimmy Barnes. He arrived from Glasgow, as a young child and they were put in government housing in Adelaide.   Many, including his father, were doomed to poverty, drink and despair. Sad to think of that.   It sounds like very poor and wasteful organisation to me.

# UNRAVELLING AUSTRALIA

## Down Under – North and South

"Down Under" is an affectionate colloquialism for Australia because we are on the underside of the globe. Perhaps also because the Aussie image projected to the world, is a swagman under an Akubra hat with corks swinging from the brim (to keep the flies off). I have never seen such a thing, except in an ad to sell beer.

If you draw a cartoon picture of the world, with people walking on it, some of us will be upside-down. Now there is a thought! Which of us are upside down? It is all relative. Relative to the ground on which we stand, we are all the right way up.

Let's say we are taking a picture from a satellite in outer-space. Who is down-under? Which countries don't we see? Well, whichever are on the other side, of course. It depends exactly where we are relative to planet Earth. And talking about relativity, according to Einstein's theory of curvature of space, if you could shoot a missile to travel forever into space, it would eventually hit you in the bum. Provided that you, and the planet are still in the same place. Which is highly unlikely.

America lies in the East, and the Middle East is to the West. The sunny side of everything is the North side and the shady side is the South. The North of Australia is tropical, and the South faces the Antarctic.

To add to my confusion, we have Christmas in mid-summer, and the seasons come in the wrong months. I say "wrong" because this is the thing that muddles me most. After all these years in Australia, I still need to think twice to know what month I am in. It just doesn't seem right that Autumn starts in March. We are truly living in an upside-down country.

We may be upside-down, but we are still spinning the same way as the Northern Hemisphere. If that were not the case, it would be very difficult for people living on the equator. The Northern and the Southern hemispheres would be spinning in opposite directions. In Australia, the sun still rises in the East and sets in the West. But it shines on the North side of my house!

When it is daytime in Australia, it is night-time in Europe and yesterday in America. To travel between Australia and America, you need to cross the International Date Line. You lose a day or gain a day, depending on whether you are coming or going. I met a girl who wasn't aware of this and travelled from Canada to Australia to spend her 21st birthday with her dad. She was disappointed to find on arrival, that her birthday was yesterday. She felt that she had lost a very important day in her life!

Tropical Australia doesn't have winter. In late summer (January, February, March) it has the "Wet" with the rivers running high, and the cyclone season. There is high humidity ashore and there are stingers in the sea. Stingers are various jelly fish which range from stinging painfully, to causing instant, agonising death. It also has crocodiles. All year round. It is worth mentioning that there are sharks in all our seas – including the infamous great white. Having said that, I should point out that shark attacks are uncommon and make headline news.

But the North is great for a summer escape from the Southern winter. The only trouble is that most of the North is thousands of miles from absolutely anywhere, so not very developed for tourism. In my opinion, there is no better place for a holiday than Australia. We have breathtaking scenery, beautiful sandy beaches, perfect places for yachting, and multiple climates. But the big thing is, you don't need to be rich. You only need a camper van.

## Down Under – East and West

East and West is a puzzle too. We live in Melbourne, which is in the South Eastern corner of Australia, in Port Philip Bay. Port Philip Bay opens out into the Bass Strait. Now I am going to look at a map, because I am getting into deep water here. All of the East coast of Australia is on the Pacific

Ocean.   Or is it?   Our ocean beaches are on the Tasman Sea.  Which is part of the South Pacific Ocean.  But it is hard to think of Melbourne, Tasmania or New Zealand being in the South Pacific.   Definitely not tropical.

All the Western Australian coast lies on the Indian Ocean. There is no confusion about that. The Atlas says so, quite clearly. I feel confused because India is known as an Eastern country. All the countries known as Eastern countries are to the West if you are in Australia.  Including the Middle East and Asia.

Part of China is north of Western Australia, and it is up in the Northern Hemisphere.  But the Chinese are trying to get everywhere.    Right now, they are planning to build a port in Darwin, to serve their trading interests.  The town council claims that the Government in Canberra isn't interested in what happens to Darwin, so why not.   Darwin is in the Top End of Australia, almost on the equator.  It actually got bombed by the Japanese in WWII, probably because there was an American base there.  I think there still is.  So in the event of a war between the US and China, it could be fought out in our Top End.  Maybe Canberra would notice that.

At the time of writing (2022), the Chinese have just signed a contract with the president of the Solomon Islands, to build a port supporting Chinese oil interests in the region. Looking at the map is a bit unsettling because all the island nations off our North coast are gradually coming under Chinese influence.  They are a long way from China but very close to Australia.  And to the South of us, there is only the Antarctic.

Looking at the brighter side of life, on the other side of the Pacific, lies the West coast of America.  From Chile in the south to Alaska in the north.   On the other side of America, lies the Atlantic Ocean.  Which is most definitely not on our shores.  In fact, to visualise where Australia is in relation to the UK, you need to picture the whole globe and its oceans. Which is quite a stretch of imagination.

When we first arrived in Australia in 1981, we flew from London, crossing Europe and landing at Dubai and Kuala Lumpa.  In other words, we flew eastwards over Europe and touched down in the Middle East, and Malaysia.  At Dubai airport, I remember looking from the plane and seeing a guard in Arab dress, sitting on a camel, with a rifle across his knees, on desert sand.  At Kuala Lumpur, we changed planes, after waiting a few hours in a shed with a few leather wallets for sale.  Nowadays, both those airports are enormous.

 Looking at a flat map of the world, you would think that the quickest way from Melbourne to the UK was straight across the Pacific, central America and the Atlantic.  But that is not the way to fly.  If you doubt me, try using a tape-measure and a world globe, to find the shortest flight paths.  And let me know if you discover anything interesting!

I have flown across the Pacific Ocean in Virgin Pacific Airlines, from Australia to Los Angeles. I don't know what route it took. Flying across the Pacific is something that most airlines avoid. There is absolutely nowhere to make an emergency landing and if a plane crashes into the wide, deep Pacific, there is little chance of ever finding it. In fact, any jet-liner would be torn apart on touching down on the sea. No survivors. So planes fly on curved flight paths up the coast of China, and then cross to Anchorage in Alaska, turning southwards into the USA.

If you want to see the Pacific, take a cruise, and visit some South Sea islands. There is something for everyone on a cruise ship. It is like staying in an unimaginably large hotel with extraordinary facilities. Not only that, a cruise is affordable, even for pensioners. But you do need to go with a friend or family, as everybody else does.

## Today is a day of Total Fire Ban

1982

When William was two weeks old, we had some friends round to celebrate, and I was at the stove, making a curry.

I heard a voice say, "You can tell he is a third baby, by the way Mary has him tucked under her arm while she's cooking,"

Well, she had a very good point. First babies can have a hard time, because their parents are so nervous around them. Parenthood becomes more relaxing with experience.

76

William was a calm and happy little kid, and I think that was because I knew what I was doing. I didn't upset him.

We moved into our Australian home in February 1982, two weeks before his second birthday. It is a long, rectangular house on a battle-axe block. Which simply means that it is behind another house and the driveway (100m long) forms the handle of the battle-axe. I loved that we were so far from the road. Safer for the children. And peaceful.

This unexpected event happened on "a day of Total Fire Ban". That was announced on the radio, and I had no idea what it meant. Well, it meant that an unbearably hot wind was going to blow. So it would be very dangerous to have a bonfire. You could burn down the neighbourhood. Not that I would think of having a bonfire, but burning off garden rubbish is a very Aussie activity. (Nowadays, we need to buy a fire pit permit for a burn-off at any day in the year. So we don't hear the Total Fire Ban thing, anymore.)

I was in the lounge room and William was playing with his Lego bricks in the family room. I suddenly noticed thick, black smoke and an acrid smell. I ran into the kitchen and found William standing on a chair, stirring something in a saucepan with a wooden spoon. He had managed to turn on the ring and he was cooking his Lego bricks! He was quite unbothered by the thick smoke. I was horrified. I flung the saucepan under the tap, turned off the ring, opened the patio door and carried William into the garden.

Not a good situation on a Fire Ban day! We had to stay in the garden, in intense heat, until the toxic fumes abated.

## The Magic Flute

1988

Music is my joy and my hobby. I learned to play the flute and the piano, both to Grade 5 music level, when I was at school. After that, as often happens, playing an instrument was an on and off thing. University, raising a family, earning money...all the usual interruptions.

When we decided to emigrate to Australia, I was a bit concerned that there might not be any classical music going on. I was also wondering whether people would be drinking wine. Wine had only recently become the in-thing in the UK. I needn't have worried on either count. The Australian wine industry was about to take off on a large scale. And shortly after our arrival, I was amazed to see a string quartet playing on a small stage in a Melbourne shopping centre.

When our kids were in primary school (we had been in Melbourne for a year) my daughter's form teacher, Margaret Fallaw, talked me into joining the Frankston Symphony Orchestra. I am glad she did, it was a lot of fun. I played in it for many years.

The Frankston and Mornington Peninsula Arts Council festival (FAMPAC) was an annual event, and our job was to accompany an opera, directed by Charles and Nina Dorning.

In their younger days, they both had very successful singing careers with the Doylie Carte Operatic Company. The result was a very professional performance.

As a child, we used to listen to the opera hour on the BBC home service, as a background to Sunday lunch. My Grandpa was brought up in Italy, and he liked to play Verdi arias on his mandolin. That was the pop music of his day! So I am very fond of opera, and when we got together with the singers for the dress-rehearsals and the performances, it was a real joy.

Now I will tell you a funny story about me. I had no idea I had caused so much consternation and amusement, until my friend Keren was telling the story recently. Thirty years after the event! On this occasion, we were performing Mozart's Magic Flute for the festival. Mozart was the Andrew Lloyd Webber of his day (1756 – 1791). His operas were popular entertainment with beautiful music and a fun story – a good night out!

The Magic Flute is a fairy tale opera. The romantic lead, Prince Tamino, is the guy with the Magic Flute. Papageno is the guy with the panpipe, played off-stage on piccolo. I was playing second flute and piccolo, and Terry was on first flute. Which means that he played most of the time and I played an occasional harmony part on the flute plus Papageno's signature "twiddly-ee!" on piccolo. The twiddly-ees were not a problem, except that in the garden scene in the second act, my part showed 84 bars rest (silence by me), followed by repeated twiddly-ees with a few rests in between.

The 84 bars rest had all sorts of stuff going on in it. General rushing about on stage (which was behind us), little spurts of orchestral music with varied tempos, and recitative. Recitative is a conversation in operatic style, mostly on one note with expression. For example:

"WHERE is PapaGENo?"

"I do not KNOW"

"I have LOST him! Where can he BEEEE!"

We had never actually rehearsed my entry, because there were no other instruments playing. I fully expected to play it at the dress rehearsal, but when we were nearly at the spot, our conductor said "We will skip the next bit, it's all recitative."

Great! I was really worried. I asked Prince Tamino for a clue. He was a friendly young Italian with a lovely voice. He said not to worry.

"When I call out Papageno, Papageno", there is a little pause and then you do your thing. We do it three times."

But I was still worried. I should point out that this was long before the internet and you-tube. Luckily, one of the violinists had borrowed the CD from the library, and she lent it to me.  Unluckily, the piccolo player on the CD had put his own interpretation on it.  He started with the usual  twiddly-ee, but played the next twiddly-ee slowly and sadly, and the third and last twiddly-ee was very slow and fading away – to indicate that Papageno's life was fading out of him.

So that is how I played it.

First twiddly-ee – our conductor raises his arms ready to bring in the orchestra.

Second twiddly-ee – I am getting slower. Our conductor gives a little twitch, but no. The time has not yet come.

Third twiddly-ee – I am drawing the twiddly-ee out as sadly as I can.

Our conductor is getting tired of holding his baton in the air. He is getting desperate. The whole orchestra is in suspense.

Keren was playing first cello right beside him.

She said, "You should have seen his face."

Keren still laughs about it.

But she is very kind and says, "It was beautiful, Mary."

# Swimming

This is a rare autumn day with hardly a ripple on Port Philip Bay. I am floating in the water, suspended in a silvery world, where sky and sea meet seamlessly, on an invisible horizon.

So I float in space, in a world that is serene and shimmering in the watery autumn sun. I feel the depths beneath me are unfathomable like the shimmering space around me. Where is the current taking me? Is it drawing me into a fantasy world where I float into the skies...Mary in the sky with diamonds?

Out of the water and back to reality...I'm walking back to the car-park in my soaking wet shirt and shorts. A young fisherman is walking beside me, towing his bright yellow skiff.

"Did you catch anything?" I ask.

"No, but my dad did," he said, smiling.

"What did he catch?"

"A few schnapper for tea. How was the water – a bit fresh?

"Yea, very fresh! But lovely."

I like the changing room at this beach. It is open to the sky; clean and airy. A brick structure painted cream, with a ledge all around to rest your bag or rest your foot to pull on your socks. There are no cubicles in beach changing rooms. The polite thing is not to look. There is a good Aussie word for looking. It's called perving. You just don't perve.

When we first migrated, I went swimming in a public pool for the first time. I was a bit taken aback when a stark-naked woman walked up to me and said, "Hello" in a warm and friendly voice. I looked at her blankly, rather alarmed.

She said, "You don't recognise me without my hat, do you?"

I'm still looking blank.

She grinned at me. "I'm the lollipop lady."

Of course she is. She's that nice lady who helps the children cross the road, at my kids' primary school.

So getting back to my changing room (which is one of the reasons I swim at this beach) it is now quite empty. Not surprising, as I'm the only person mad enough to swim in this late autumn afternoon. I love the cream walls ending under a blue sky instead of under some grubby roof. But I can think of several countries where there would be sexually frustrated men jumping up the outside walls to peek over!

I don't love the shower – it produces a trickle of very cold water so forget it. I'll get changed, do my shopping and go home. And have a long, hot shower to get my circulation back.

# AUSTRALIA'S HISTORICAL MOMENTS

Australia does not have a lot of official history.  Aussie kids aren't forced to learn the dates of a thousand years of battles and Kings and Queens. There are no medieval cathedrals, no castles, no stately homes, no Roman remains. So what are the events that everybody knows about?

Well, the most renowned 'historical events' are really a very odd selection. And Ned Kelly is the oddest of all.  Ned Kelly was a 'bush-ranger' . He was an outlaw, who had to leave town and live in the bush with his brothers because he was in the habit of robbery with violence. The thing which makes Ned different from other thugs of his time, was that he wore a thing like a small metal dustbin over his head. This makeshift helmet had a door for his face. He was finally caught and hanged and there is a small museum devoted to his memory, built on the site of the siege and capture of his gang in Glenrowan, near Wangaratta, Victoria.

I think Ned Kelly is Australia's substitute for Guy Fawkes. He also, is not remembered for a successful venture. We

85

don't let off fireworks to celebrate Ned Kelly but, in Victoria, nobody would fail to identify a picture of his tin helmet.

Ned Kelly was hanged in 1880, at the age of 25. He is quoted as saying, "Ah well, I suppose it has come to this! Such is life!"

Anzac Day is another oddity of Australian history. This is a Remembrance Day for the Anzacs, who were the Australians and New Zealanders who suffered terrible losses in the first world war, on the beaches in Turkey. Anzac Day is a Public Holiday which is strictly observed.

Now Australians served in both world wars, and were conscripted to serve with the Americans in Vietnam. Yet remembrance of our war heroes is focused on the ill-fated Dardanelles campaign of World War 1. To the extent that our Prime Minister (or his representative) has to go and weep over the war graves in Turkey, on Anzac Day. The Turks must be puzzled by it.

We attended our son William's Passing-out Parade as an Army Reservist, and there again, the Brigadier managed to mention the Anzacs, and only the Anzacs, in his speech.

## Australia Day or Invasion Day?

The Aboriginal people (who now prefer to be known as First Nation) are indignant that they are the forgotten people in the history of Australia. They are right about that. Not only forgotten, but swept under the carpet.    Australia Day is celebrated on the 26<sup>th</sup> of January, the anniversary of the arrival of the First Fleet.   Marching bands and Flag Raising being the order of the day.   Now the First Nation are renaming it "Invasion Day".  It was not initially an armed invasion, but it was the beginning of a colony for Britain, and the end of freedom for the Aboriginals.   They lost their homeland.   They had no concept of material possession, and yet they were totally dispossessed.   They lost their way of life, and it was not replaced.   They have suffered more than two hundred  years of government policies which have treated them like vermin.   And now they are campaigning for Reconciliation with the white people of Australia.

On arriving in Australia in 1981, our children were not happy at being called "Abo" in school (because of their suntanned complexions).    Heidi was quite shocked that they thought she was Aboriginal, she couldn't see the connection.   The kids who were taunting her, had more than likely never seen an aboriginal.

Later, when she started at a private school, which had boarders from Asia, I asked if she was having any trouble with the "Abo" thing.

"Oh no!" she said, "If someone calls me Abo at the bus stop, I just tell them that I am not Australian and they don't bother me anymore."

Right now, in 2022, attitudes are changing and people are much more enlightened about the plight of the indigenous people.

## Colonisation: the shocking truth

Until today (October 2022), I always thought that Australia was lucky to have been colonised by the British and not the Spanish (who had a brutal reputation for colonisation). I was wrong. The "First Nation" is now gaining a voice. A new 3-part television series, "The Australian Wars" (by multi-award winning, indigenous film maker, Rachel Perkins) has just been put to air on SBS. Extensively researched by universities, looking at official records and oral histories, this documentary reveals a horrendous story. In the nineteenth century, thousands of aboriginals were slaughtered to make room for sheep and cattle stations. Men, women and children were shot, and their bodies burned. How could this happen? The answer, is that they were black, stark naked and dangerous, and so could easily be labelled "subhuman" and treated as vermin. They were also very troublesome. The stigma still lives on, in post-colonial Australia today.

*Ironically, many of the settlers had migrated because they lost their small-holdings to the new wool industry. Landlords found that one man and his dog could look after six hundred sheep. So no need to bother with tenants anymore. They arrived in Australia, after a long and unpleasant voyage, hoping for a new chance at life – only to find that the natives were trying to drive them out. Just like in the old cowboy movies where the "injuns" were always the bad guys.*

*There's colonisation for you! I remember playing cowboys and injuns with bows and arrows made of bamboo, when I was a little kid.*

# Deprivation of the First Nation

Australia looked to North America as a model for colonisation, putting the indigenous people into reservations, where they lived in poverty with no hope of improvement. Another scheme learned from the Americans was taking indigenous children from their parents and putting them into school camps, foster care or domestic service. The idea was to make them forget their own language and lifestyle. This is now known as the "Lost Generation". In America, it is called the "Broken Feathers". All this was supposedly to "protect" them. In reality, it broke them. Snatched from their homes, without paperwork to make their families traceable, frequently imprisoned for minor crimes, and devoid of any proper direction.

This is still going on. Children or grandchildren can be snatched away by child-services without proof of neglect. 16,816 Aboriginal children were reportedly put in out-of-home care in 2016. Many were being lovingly cared for by grandparents because their mothers were suffering substance abuse.

Believe it or not, the indigenous people were not classified as Australian citizens until 1967. This meant that they had no human rights. It meant that, when the South Australian desert was used for Atom Bomb tests by the British army in the 1950s, aboriginal casualties were listed under "flora and fauna" (plants and animals). Presumably some bureaucrat looked at the census (which, by law, did not include any indigenous people) and proclaimed the land was uninhabited and available for nuclear fall-out. But it was not.

## Our Australian Citizenship Ceremony

In 1988, Australia commemorated the bi-centenary of the arrival of the First Fleet. The celebrations included the World Expo in Brisbane (we went up to Brisbane specially and it was great) and a parade of square-rigged training ships (from all over the world) on Sydney Harbour. We happened to have our Australian Citizenship ceremony then, and so we were treated to a dinner party by the local Lions Club and a present of an old penny (to initiate us into the good old Australian gambling game of "two up") and a pottery gum-nut baby to hang on the wall. And we swore allegiance to the Queen. This came as a surprise, as I can't ever remember being asked to swear allegiance in the UK, and I did not feel that I was changing anything. Still my Queen!

*I swear by Almighty God that I will be faithful and bear true allegiance to Her Majesty Elizabeth the Second, Queen of Australia, Her heirs and successors according to law, and that I will faithfully observe the laws of Australia and fulfil my duties as an Australian citizen.*

*Incidentally, the present-day Oath of Citizenship does not mention the Queen. This new oath was slipped in with the Republican Referendum. And it was kept, even though the republic was rejected. The new oath is cleverly worded to fit all situations.*

The new oath  (under God is optional):
*From this time forward, under God,*

*I pledge my loyalty to Australia and its people,*

*whose democratic beliefs I share,*

*whose rights and liberties I respect, and*

*whose laws I will uphold and obey.*

# Captain James Cook

Right now (2022) James Cook is being made a scapegoat for all the sins committed by the colonials.  This is one of the problems of not teaching history.  It gets invented.  Now that a consciousness is developing about the plight of the indigenous people (nobody cared a damn before), I am hearing this from people who should know better: "Cook was a horrible man; he shot all the aborigines".  I noticed an interesting question on the internet, "How many aborigines were there before Cook shot them all?"

1. *Nobody knows how many aboriginal people were in Australia in 1770, and the Endeavour was an exploratory vessel with a small scientific task force, not a warship.*

2. *They weren't shot by Cook. They were destroyed by colonisation.  But that started 18 years after Cook's discoveries.  Today, only 3.2% of Australians are aboriginal.*

Like many seafarers of the time, Cook came from a humble, rural environment. His father was a Northumbrian farm labourer, who married a Yorkshire lass and settled near Whitby. James Cook was born in the West Riding of Yorkshire, on the 27th October 1728. He began his seafaring career with the Walkers of Whitby, when he was fourteen years old. The Walkers were a devout Quaker family, with strict rules of behaviour for their apprentices.

James did a few years as a common seaman and was raised to be mate of one of Mr Walker's ships. He took command of a collier (coastal coal-carrying sailing barque) in the wild waters of the North Sea, which was to be a valuable experience for him. But when hostilities broke out between Britain and France in 1755, James volunteered as an Able Seaman in the Royal Navy. Join the navy and see the world! After distinguishing himself in the Quebec war, he became a known expert in navigation and chart-making. And, would you believe, the navy used Whitby colliers for voyages of exploration! So James was the man for the job.

In other words, he was of good character and an exemplary office, known for keeping a healthy and happy ship. And he tried as much as possible, not to harm the native peoples they encountered, throughout the voyage.

Was Cook the first explorer to find Australia? No, but the others had not found anything to like. Australia is a huge island with 34,000 km (21,000 miles) of coastline. The Endeavour was the first ship to explore the East Coast, and found it good and fertile. In fact, most Australians live on the East side today.

## Why British? How come?

Here, we are almost diametrically on the opposite side of the world from the UK. To be exact, New Zealand's Antipodes Islands are diametrically opposed to London, being at Latitude 52 degrees south and longitude 180. So you might well ask, how on Earth did Australia and New Zealand fall into the hands of the British?

The answer is that this was the result of a chain of very quirky decisions made by interesting characters in the 18th century. You could say that it happened by pure serendipity. It could, so very easily, never have happened at all.

## Quirky Decision 1 – a bid for fame and fortune

Alexander Dalrymple, a Scottish aristocrat and already famous for scientific discovery and a major mover and shaker in the East India Company, had a plan to take command of a ship, with a sailing master (a bit like a yacht charter) and seek out the Unknown Great Southern Land, *Terra Australis Incognita,* and thus achieve fame and fortune by opening up trade with a hitherto unknown civilisation. To do this, he required one of his Majesty's ships, and he expected to get one, as he was a geographer for the Navy.

*The ancient Greeks believed there must be an undiscovered continent attached to the South Pole, to balance Europe on the North Pole. Philosophers still clung to this idea, although there was no proof. In fact, the continents are mere eruptions on the skin of planet Earth, so they do not need balancing. Possibly the Greeks thought of the world as a hollow sphere. Seeing as the Americas were completely missing from Ptolemy's maps, it is odd that geographers in the 18th century didn't pause and think a bit.*

The First Lord of the Admiralty, Sir Edward Hawke, absolutely refused to give Dalrymple a command, saying, "I would rather suffer my right hand to be cut off than trust any of his Majesty's ships to a person who had not been properly bred to the service (the Royal Navy)."

## Quirky Decision 2 - a secret agenda

The Royal Society was pushing for a scientific expedition to make measurements of the transit of Venus across the sun. This was to help calculate the distance from Earth to the sun. It meant sending a ship to an island off the coast of West Africa to set up an observatory and make measurements. The ship was then to cross the Atlantic, round Cape Horn and explore the South Pacific.

James Cook was chosen to command the vessel, and promoted to Lieutenant for the purpose. This voyage of exploration took three years. At any time during those three years, His Majesty's Barque Endeavour could easily have been lost at sea, without ever bringing back the charts of

Australia and the South Pacific. They were out in the blue, with no friendly ships to take dispatches or letters home, and no port of call for provisions or repairs. It was a case of self-survival. It is an absolute miracle that they survived shipwreck, and were not stuck in an Antarctic ice field or slaughtered by Maori warriors in New Zealand.

For some time, European maritime powers had been hotly contesting for new places to colonise. So the voyage of exploration in the South Pacific had to be top secret! The voyage of the Endeavour was officially a scientific expedition, put forward by the Royal Society. Endeavour carried a scientific team, led by Joseph Banks, a keen botanist and zoologist. At 25 years old Banks was a wealthy man, and he put ten thousand pounds into the expedition, which was a small fortune in those days. So the mission was put into Cook's secret orders, to be opened after observing the transit of Venus.

Above all, Cook was to explore "The Southern Continent", and failing that, to survey New Zealand and see whether it was joined to the mythical continent.

*New Zealand was assumed to be a headland sticking out of Terra Australis Incognita. What we now call Australia, was accepted as a Southern Land but did not solve the problem of finding the unknown Southern civilisation.*

On the voyage of the Endeavour, Mr Cook (he was only a lieutenant, not a captain at that time) completed a very accurate mapping of both north and south islands of New Zealand and declared that it was definitely not attached to the "imaginary continent". He also sailed as far south as he could, but was stopped by ice-floes which made further advancement much too dangerous.

*For James Cook, looking for a continent which he soon lost belief in, was the bane of his life. He had to battle the Antarctic ice fields in freezing cold conditions, in a wooden barque, under sail.*

## Quirky decision 3 – Botany Bay

It was Cook's own decision to carry on in a North-Westerly direction for the journey home. And that is how he came to chart the East coast of Australia – an entirely new discovery. Totally unknown vegetation, extraordinary wild-life, and people who disappeared into the bush whenever the Endeavour appeared.

The Endeavour stopped for exactly a week at Botany Bay (Sunday 29th April 1770 – Sunday 6th May 1770). Cook was not able to make contact with the natives, who kept their distance and could not be lured. They were stark naked and only wore paint – no jewellery. Trading was not an option. They weren't interested and they were very busy fishing from simple canoes.

Cook recorded in his log:

*"The Earth and the sea provide them with all the things necessary for life, they covet not Magnificent Houses,*

*Household stuff etc, and live in a warm and fine Climate and enjoy a very wholesome Air, so that they have very little need of clothing... In short, they seemed to set no value on anything we gave them, nor would they ever part with anything of their own for any one article we could offer them."*

However, colonisation was a possibility: fresh water, fertile land, and no sign of civilisation.

## Shipwreck and Tribulation

The Endeavour sailed slowly northwards, charting the waters of "the place we now call home". She sailed right through the beautiful Whitsunday islands (so-named by Cooke because they arrived there on Whitsunday) and continued northwards, blissfully unaware of the Great Barrier reef to seaward of her position. A satellite photo of Earth would have come in useful! The linesman reported deep water, and a few seconds later, they crashed into the reef. All hands to the pumps, and the ship was leaking fast.

Miraculously, they saved the situation and managed to beach her and make repairs. Cook named the place Cape Tribulation. "This was where all my tribulations began," said Cook. But the accident put an end to their exploration of Australia because they had to make for the nearest ship-yard, and that was in Batavia (Java) – arriving there on 11th October 1770. They had been at sea for more than two years, without losing a man to disease. In those days, ships could expect to lose half the crew to scurvy, but there was no scurvy on board with Cook in command. He was a firm believer in pickled cabbage and other green vegies to combat scurvy. In fact, Luncheon Bay on Whitsunday Island was named after a boat excursion to seek greens for the ship's cook.

Unfortunately, although the Batavia shipyard did excellent work, one third of the Endeavour's complement were to die of "Batavia Fever" as a result of the visit. Many were infected and few recovered. Some died quickly, others lingered for months in a state of weakness before they passed away. Later Cook was to hear that the disease had infected all the Dutch ships that called at Batavia at that time. An all too familiar story, considering Covid-19.

After rounding the Cape of Good Hope, Endeavour returned safely to England in July 1771. They had been at sea for exactly three years. James Cook had left a heavily pregnant wife and three children in London. He returned to find that the newborn had died and so had their only daughter. In those days, infant mortality was all too common. But Joseph Banks was knighted for his contribution to science, and Cook was promoted to Commander and given a hero's welcome. I find it amazing that even though he was navigating entirely by the sun, the stars and the moon, James Cook's charts had the accuracy of a GPS! That shows great thoroughness, and dedication.

Cook was under orders from the Admiralty, and the Admiralty was influenced by the rich and powerful. The merchants wanted to be first in the race to find new territories, undiscovered civilisations and places to grow profitable crops. Australia did not fit into that scenario. For his next voyage he was sent to find the fabled, great Southern Land. Possibly jealousy prompted Dalrymple to persist in not acknowledging that Australia (then known as New Holland) could indeed be the missing continent. He maintained that Cook did not look hard enough. So Cook, ever the perfectionist, charted the Antarctic in a wooden collier built for the North Sea coal trade. With his faithful and devoted crew.

## Cook's third, and last voyage

The tea merchants wanted to find a short cut to the Pacific, through the Arctic, instead of having to sail via the South Pacific to get to China. There was rumoured to be a Northwest passage joining the North Atlantic to the North Pacific. It was on this voyage of exploration, that he was chopped into little pieces by the natives of Hawaii.

Captain Cook never returned to Botany Bay. His other two great voyages of exploration in the Pacific Ocean, did not include Australia.

Although he did stop for a few days in Van Diemen's land (now Tasmania), in January 1777 (on his third voyage to the Pacific). His small ship was carrying a cargo of farm animals. It must have been very inconvenient. They went ashore to find grass to feed the farm animals. This incident was quite bizarre, as was Cook's to-do list for voyage. He had been given the job of dropping off cattle and pigs, into possible new territories, to breed and multiply of their own accord.

I can understand the thinking behind this. The Pacific Islands were seen to be totally lacking in the essentials for a good British dinner. In fact, there were no hooved animals at all. So how were the settlers going to feed themselves?

*Another thing on the to-do list, was taking home a young and distinguished Pacific Islander called Omai. He was the second Pacific Islander ever, to visit Europe. (Omai was brought out on the Adventure, with Cook's second Pacific exploration). For two years Omai had been the darling of the social elite in London, thanks to Sir Joseph Banks. Omai even had his portrait painted by Sir Joshua Reynolds (it sold at a record price for a portrait in 2001).*

Cook went ashore with Omai and a working party:

*"We were agreeably surprised, at the place where we were cutting wood, with a visit from some of the natives. They came out of the woods without showing any fear and with the greatest confidence imaginable...I showed them two pigs (a boar and two sows) I had brought ashore to leave in the woods and the instant they saw them they grabbed them by the ears like a dog and were for carrying them off immediately. With no other view we could perceive but to kill them."*

*Omai wanted to show off what a musket could do, and shot*

at a target. The natives dropped everything and ran away in terror. Cook found a sheltered spot for the pigs and left them there.

In all three voyages of exploration, Cook was stymied by dangerously icy conditions. It was soon quite clear to him, that there was no maritime passage through the polar regions, due to the climate, but he had the frustrating situation of having orders to find one.

All quotations from James Cook's log entries are taken from:

James Cook, The Journals, Prepared from James Cook's original manuscripts by J.C. Beaglehole for the Hakluyt Society , 1953-67, Selected and edited by Philip Edwards, Penguin Classics. ISBN-13: 978-0-140-43647-1, ISBN-10: 0-14043647-2

# Quirky Decision 4 – The First Fleet

Australia, and in particular, Botany Bay was marked on the chart as uninhabited country with potential for future colonisation. As a result, 18 years later Captain Arthur Philip arrived with the First Fleet and a cargo of convicts: men, women and children. A strange decision based on very little information. But it was the foundation of the colony we now call Australia.

The passage of the First Fleet was an epic voyage and a world first – eleven vessels carrying about 1,487 people and stores had travelled for 252 days for more than 15,000 miles (24,000 km) without losing a ship. Only forty-eight people died on the journey, a death rate of just over three per cent.

Captain Philip's mission was quite extraordinary. He was the governor of a colony which he was to build, using the convicts as his labour force. In other words, he was to land in Botany Bay and create a new British colony from scratch. When he stepped ashore in Botany Bay, he "read himself in" exactly as if he were taking command of a ship in the Royal Navy. Indeed, his orders said that he was putting the whole of "New Holland", as it was then called, under British rule.

No guidelines as to what to do about the natives. That problem was not taken into consideration by the planners in London. During Philip's term of office, the colony was only beginning. But in the long-term, this complete disregard for the natives was disastrous, and resulted in much loss of life and a very bitter and fearful relationship on both sides. Not so disastrous for the wool-merchants, however. They achieved their plan.

## Captain Matthew Flinders

*It was Captain Matthew Flinders who, in 1801, after making a complete circuit of the coast of New Holland (starting and ending in the Bass strait) proposed to rename our country as Terra Australis or Australia, the great southern land. Which solved the whole problem, including the problem of calling a British territory New Holland.*

# JABILUKA BLOCKADE

## 1998

Sydney, Melbourne, Brisbane, Adelaide and Perth are cities which, even when you've lived in them for years, give no hint that the rest of Australia is almost uninhabited. There is no sign of the dreaded bush (apart from the occasional lethal snake or spider). Houses are getting bigger and bigger, school fees are getting higher and higher, the streets are crowded with the latest cars from Japan and Germany, and it all seems quite normal.

Darwin is different. In Darwin, you know you are in Australia — you couldn't be anywhere else. Darwin is one of the last outposts of a bygone age. Or perhaps Darwin is the real Australia — without the illusion of First World prosperity.

I went to Darwin at the invitation of my daughter. Heidi was there because she had been involved in the Jabiluka protest against Uranium mining in the Kakadu National Park, the year before. She had just graduated with an Environmental Management degree, from RMIT (Royal Melbourne Institute of Technology). The Mirarr people (the traditional owners of the land) had appealed to the student unions at Melbourne University and RMIT, to support a blockade to prevent a new uranium mine on their sacred land (also known as the sick country).

It was a very "full on" experience where the protesters experienced confrontation from the local police and uranium miners. Heidi travelled from Melbourne by bus (a journey of 3,753 kilometres) to join the protest camp in bushland near Jabiru.

"We were tipped off that the miners were going to start work. Our idea of a peaceful protest was that some of us would sit down in the path of their excavators and then others would climb up and chain themselves to them. That didn't happen. The miners were accompanied by police with big guns and bullet proof gear. They physically dragged us off the road. Of course, we were wearing light summer clothing. My T-shirt rucked up and my back was all grazed. It was a big shock, and very frightening.

" A peaceful protest in Darwin was arranged as a publicity stunt. This was not so bad. It was prearranged with the police to observe the rules for peaceful protest and have the choice of whether or not to be arrested.

"Some students were afraid they would be banned from teaching if they had a criminal record," says Heidi, "It was an emotional situation, because there was peer pressure not to leave.

"Someone made up a little song, on the spur of the moment, and he and I sang it to the TV cameras:

*We are fine*

*We are super*

*And we will stop*

*Jabiluka!"*

*Jabiluka is one of the world's largest undeveloped uranium deposits. Over 500 people were arrested in the course of the blockade, which went on the for eight months. There was world-wide support for the action, including the European government and the World Heritage Committee. This was part of a major environmental and cultural campaign, with legal battles going on for years and years. The Blockade effectively stopped the miners going in, but the legal battle went on a lot longer. It was a complex issue involving: the rights of traditional owners of the land (Yvonne Margarula was arrested for trespass on her own land); anti-nuclear action; and environmental protection. It was party political too. Whenever Hawke's Labor party was in, development of the Jabiluka mine was suspended, but Howard's Liberal governments put uranium mining right back to the top of their agenda. Nonetheless, very few voters around the nation were aware, so not really an election issue.*

# 1999 – my visit to Darwin

The protestors had to return 6 months later to face charges. Heidi's case came up on December 28th 1998, so we missed her at Christmas, as she was driving up to Darwin with her boyfriend. After being sentenced to weed a football oval (in intense heat) for 4 days, she decided to stay on and help out at the local environmental protest office. And then she gave me a call and said, "Why don't you come up now, we are leaving soon for Perth.

After a six-hour flight, I arrived in Darwin. The air was so humid that I wasn't sure whether it was raining or not. In fact, it wasn't. The heat was almost unbearable. Darwin is 10 degrees South of the equator and this was the tail end of the hot and humid wet season. Very tropical.

I was staying in a resort because, with only seven days' notice, it was much cheaper to book a Qantas package than a flight. And it was nice to have a swimming pool. Although I was a bit taken aback to see a green snake fall out of a palm tree, and wiggle about in the safety-net suspended above the pool!

Heidi was staying in a student "share-house" near Darwin Uni. In other words, it was a rental with a group of students in it. It was an old, timber house, built in traditional style, standing on very tall stilts, to keep the rooms above possible flood waters in "the Wet".

The first, and only, floor had a veranda around it and no windowpanes. This allowed the air to circulate, with the aid of ceiling fans. Tall palm trees, thickly planted, provided shade and privacy. Mosquito nets kept the mossies away. Ceiling fans and walls made only of fly-wire are not uncommon in the Northern Territory. It is an arrangement that really suits the climate. I found that I coughed all night if I slept with air-conditioning — sleeping with ceiling fans is better.

We visited some friends who lived in another old-fashioned house on stilts. All the other houses in the street were modern. Apparently, it was the only house in the street left standing after Cyclone Tracey devasted Darwin in 1974. We were shown an aerial photograph of the area, taken after the Cyclone. Saved by a gigantic banyan tree in the garden. The rest of the houses were flattened. I walked inside the banyan's sheltering root-walls, and found a very fat lizard, resting on a branch.

In Darwin, the indigenous people are to be seen every day, sitting in little groups on the pavement, talking in their language and drinking cheap wine out of bottles held in paper bags. Usually the group consists of women in cotton frocks and one man in jeans, T-shirt, and a clean, white bandage — possibly a fracture resulting from a drunken dispute.

One such group of indigenous, turned up in the garden, one evening. They were with an older couple that Heidi knew. They had come to the door one day, and asked for fish-hooks. Heidi was a little nervous, but they seemed OK and she gave them some. In the evening, after their fishing, they dropped by and gave her a barramundi — which is a big fish with a delicate taste, an up-market meal! After that, she went fishing with the woman occasionally.

On this occasion, introductions were done — my cousin, my nephew etc. The nephew had a broken arm in a clean white sling. We chatted a little bit, but were in a hurry to go into town for a restaurant meal.

When Heidi returned, her woman friend was sleeping on the bottom board of the flight of steps to the rooms. She had brought a Police summons for her nephew. She wanted Heidi to read it for her. It was for urinating in a public place. This is a bit of an issue, because the aboriginal people come into Darwin and "Long-grass" i.e. they just lie down and sleep in the grass in the parkland by the cliffs. If there are toilets, they are usually locked at night, to keep them clean.

Unfortunately, the "blackfellas" (as they call themselves) who come into Darwin may be there for drinking — it's the addicts who come into town, and as they have a low alcohol tolerance, they get into trouble.

Heidi felt bad about rushing off, without asking the purpose of the visit. Anyway, the next day, she went down to the courthouse with the woman, to help her.

Early one morning, I went for a prebreakfast stroll with my camcorder, through the park overlooking the navy moorings. The path was blocked by a little group of aboriginal people, drinking and laughing in the pleasant morning sun. I asked if I could film them and if they would talk to the camera. Just one of the women spoke English, she translated to the others and asked if it was for television. I said, "No, just for my family in Melbourne." They were all right with that, but I noticed the paper bags quickly go behind their backs — they could be convicted for drinking. She introduced all her companions with exact family relationships and said they had come into town to pass the time for a while. Then she asked if I could give them money for smokes . I showed her that I only had enough cash on me for a coffee. "That's OK, go have your coffee." One of the women had a bad smoker's cough.

*When I showed this movie to my family, we happened to have a visitor from India. He was very surprised that the aborigines didn't understand English.  The reason for his surprise that he thought education was available to everyone in Australia. That is a very good point.*

These people wandering into Darwin are not far removed from the bush, even though they no longer wander around naked with boomerangs. They have much in common with the little bushman in that whimsically hilarious South African movie "The God's must be Crazy" or the tribes of the Amazon rain-forest who wake up one morning to find that their whole world has been transformed into wood-chip.

*(2022 note: The brutality perpetrated by police, nowadays highlighted by the "Black Lives Matter" movement, has been echoed in our First Nation's struggle in Australia).*

The police are not entirely to blame. The fault lies in Federal Government failing to provide proper aid to rescue the aborigines from their situation. This is a job for the federal (Australian) government — it can't be left to town councils or state governments. They have neither the knowledge nor the resources. But of course, rescuing Aborigines from alcohol addiction, the wife-beating resulting from substance abuse, the unemployment that results from not speaking English and just plain prejudice — is not a vote catcher. And it certainly doesn't win corporate brownie points.

When I see TV advertising for World Vision, asking Australians to "adopt" an African or Indonesian child by sending a contribution, I wonder why we aren't being asked to help out our own indigenous people. I suppose the answer is simple. Australia is not a third world country, so we are expected to be capable of looking after our own. But that is not being done. Apart from a few dedicated volunteers, nobody wants to know about the indigenous people.

Darwin Markets: We went to a market to buy some vegetables. And because you just haven't experienced Darwin if you miss out on the open-air markets. Heidi had a friend with a stall there, selling homegrown organic fruit and veggies.

Darwin has a long-established Chinese population, dating back to the goldrush in the 1870s. and their stands are what really make Darwin markets different from other markets. I was fascinated by a basket of Darwin mud-crabs, crawling around with their legs tied. This is a black coloured crab, with a shell about 15 cm wide. They are also sold live in Vietnamese shopping centres in Melbourne.

My favourite souvenir of Darwin market is a video clip of me tasting Tum-yum soup for the first time! It was a lot spicier than I expected. But a glass of fresh mango juice from another Chinese stall, was great to put the fire out!

Keeping cool:  When we were out and about, I took every opportunity to go for a dip and cool down.  But my trouble with swimming in water-holes is that I am not a very strong swimmer, so I usually found myself swept into a corner with an overweight lizard. I wasn't the only one struggling with the heat.  Heidi had adopted a "Heinz 57 variety" terrier pup in Ceduna in South Australia, on the way to Darwin.  She was a stray, and had outstayed her welcome at the pound.  Heidi just had to save her. A lovely addition to the family.  She was named Tjillyi on account of her silvery coat. Tjillyi is the Pitjantjatjara name for the silvery-leaved saltbush which grows on the South Australian foreshore.   In the steamy heat of Darwin, Tjillyi was on constant lookout for a shady corner, stepping into the doorway of every shop we passed.  Once Tjillyi disappeared and we found her sheltering under a table, where someone was selling tickets for something-or-the-other.

At the student share-house, they cooled down by filling an old-fashioned bath-tub in the garden!

# BIRD TALK AND DOGGY TALES

## Why don't you talk to me?

Who says that humans are the only animals with speech? That is nonsense. I am quite sure the magpie that regularly visits my blueberry bush, was talking about it this morning. Now the magpie has a beautiful singing voice but that wasn't the voice she was using. She was talking about exactly how many berries are ripe today.

Parrots definitely have the power of speech. They have tongues like ours, but above all, they understand about speech. They have got the concept. I have had conversations with parrots that go way beyond "Hello cocky".

I was in the Public Library in Guildford, UK, when a little voice said, "Why don't you talk to me?" I looked behind me to find a budgie in a cage. Now a budgie is a very social creature and in Australia, they usually fly in thousands, as great clouds of birds. Admittedly, this budgie may have been taught the words and the sad Inflexion of loneliness. But it couldn't do that, if it didn't have the concept. The budgie knows that speech is for communication.

Now picture this: the eclectus parrots of the North Queensland tropical forests, live high up in the tallest trees. They are a very unusual parrot. The female is bright red and makes a nest in a hole in the tree trunk. Then she sits in it with her red breast making her very visible to male eclectus parrots. The males are green, so they can fly above the treetops without being seen by predators, such as birds of prey. They come courting, and when she lays her eggs, they all rush round to feed her and help feed the chicks. And they are giving the same attention to other ladies too.

So the eclectus parrot has been living a life a long way away from human beings, for thousands of years. The parrot is one of the earliest inventions of nature as we know it. Yet, one of them started up a conversation with me in a zoo (Rainbow Jungle Parrot Breeding Centre, Kalbarri, W.A.) She said, "Not much of a crowd here today is there?" And she was right. So I said, "There isn't". So she said, "So how are you?" So I said, "Good, thank you." And she said, "Have a nice day".

We live in a house with a long driveway. In the street where I live, this is called a battle-axe block, because the garden is a rectangle on the end of a long driveway at right angles. My garden and my driveway form two sides of the block between me and the street. We form the second layer of housing.

My neighbour was keeping hens but kept forgetting to close the gate. So I would be driving down my driveway at 4 kilometres an hour behind three hens clucking to each other, like ladies on a morning exercise walk.   I know what they were saying!

"Don't take any notice of all that hooting that is going on behind us."

"Of course not, dear, I never take any notice of annoying humans in cars."

"If we walk a little faster, do you think she'll stop hooting?"

And the other hen said, "No, don't bother."

## Our Pup Max

1992: Max was a present for William, on his twelfth birthday. The children and I  went to  the Pearcedale animal shelter, to pick a pup.

It was Max who picked William.  There were some very ugly dogs who bared their teeth and growled threateningly, but when we came to Max's enclosure, he immediately singled out  William, jumped up and down excitedly, and gazed lovingly with soft brown eyes.  We had to have him.

I told the nice lady that we wanted him, but I was worried that our block was enclosed by a farm-gate, and there was a groove under the gate, big enough for a pup to squeeze out.  So I asked if we could reserve him for tomorrow.  The answer was no, you have to take him now.  I had no idea then, but I since realised that he would have outstayed his welcome. The shelter pets have a limited tenancy before they are put down. I am so glad we rescued him. He was a beautiful friend and family member, for fourteen years.

I paid $80 for his vaccination certificate and a lead, and we took him home. My husband said,

"Is he ours?"

"Yes"

"OK."

Max was 6 months old and full of beans. In the afternoon, William was playing doubles in a tennis tournament at Bruce Park. Max watched every match with absolute devotion.

Bharat built him a kennel in the carport, using bricks from an old incinerator. It was decided that Max would be an outdoor dog.

Max continued to show his undying love for his new master, in the next few days. A patio window was left open a few inches, and unfortunately, William left his brand-new school shoes (brown leather lace-ups), right by the opening. Max dragged one of them out through the gap, and chewed on it happily.

For his next effort, he selected William's T-shirts from the washing line, and chewed them up. It all goes to show what a good sense of smell dogs have!

Max was officially a kelpie cross on account of a set of very pointy, kelpie teeth.   The kelpie is a popular Aussie sheep dog, derived from border collie ancestors.   His legs were too long, and his ears flopped over, so he wasn't quite right. You could call him a common-or-garden black dog.

He demonstrated his kelpie characteristics by :

1.  Trying to round up 4-wheel drives by running round them, when they were passing the house.  He may have been looking for his previous owners.

2.  Biting up the garden hose into neat one-foot lengths, when left home alone.

3.  He had a visiting kelpie friend, who looked very much like him.  We called him the freedom-fighter, because he came into our garden and bit off Max's collar. Plus the two of them indulged in some team work, pulling sheets off the washing tree. He must have sniffed out Max from afar.

4.  The strange incident of the trashed bedroom.  This is what happened:

    I don't know how he managed it, but my son Jon accidentally broke a small window in his sister's bedroom.  We removed the broken glass. The next morning, I was puzzled to hear Max barking in the house (remember, he was an outdoor dog). I went to investigate. Max had jumped through the window, and well and truly trashed the room.

He had chewed up Heidi's brand-new, wide-brimmed sunhat, torn her feather pillow apart, and shortened the curtains – which now hung with a jagged edge, half-way up the window- panes. Then he apparently forgot how he got in (as dogs often do) and sat and barked until he was rescued.

Our cats were horrified to find themselves living with a dog. They somehow managed to organise a territorial divide. The cats in the front garden (accessible through the cat-flap in the back door); and the dog in the much larger back-garden. The result was that the birds returned to the back-garden, which they had abandoned on account of the cats. Max was not interested in chasing birds. I saw him gnawing on a meaty bone, with a magpie on the other end of it!

The power of language: According to the neurologist Oliver Sacks, in his book "The Man who mistook his Wife for a Hat", dogs don't so much learn words, they connect to our vibes. This is not surprising, as they are pack animals and need to communicate to hunt. Orcas have a large part of their brain devoted to interconnecting with each other. A baby learns language from its mother, aided by a very close connection to her. My mother had an uncanny way of reading my mind, even when I was all grown up and trying desperately to think of something else.

We had some friends round for a swim, and I was in the other end of the pool.  Max came out of the house and sat down in the sun.  I pointed and called out:

"Don't sit in the sun, Max,  go over there and sit under that bush."

He obeyed, to everyone's amazement.

The exterminator:  I made a lunch-time appointment with the exterminator, to come in and  remove a wasp-nest, from a tree near the front-door. Max was very afraid of anyone carrying tools or a broom, and could react badly.  I suspect he was a failed sheepdog (their trainers use brooms to guide them).  I had warned the exterminators not to get out of their car before I shut up the dog, but that plan did not work out.  We both arrived at 1pm sharp, but he went down the driveway ahead of me. And jumped out of the car.  Max started barking sharply.

*"Ouch! He bit my bum!"*

*"I told you not to get out",*

*"I was watching the black dog – it was the other one!"*

Tjillyi, Heidi's terrier, had decided to back up her friend Max, and join in the action.  Fortunately, no blood was drawn. Only some wounded trousers.

The Gardener: I mentioned that Max was classified as a Kelpie on account of his teeth. Kelpies have very sharp teeth. I had my neighbour's gardener do a job for me, and he decided to tie Max up. He attached a long, thick rope to Max's lead. When I came home, Max lying was down quietly, at the end of the rope. The gardener said that he hoped I did not mind his tying the dog up. I pointed out that he wasn't tied up. He had bitten through his lead. The gardener did not come again. I am glad he did not. My neighbour's two dogs ate snail-bait and died.

The Jehovah's witnesses, 2004: When Max was getting a bit elderly and rheumatic, we had a visit from a Jehovah's witness couple, giving out the "Watch Tower". The wife had a flowery dress and a parasol. When they were leaving, my husband scolded Max.

"What were you thinking, Max, letting those people in?"

Poor old Max. He limped round the corner and the next we knew, he was barking fiercely. I hurried to the driveway. Max had the man pinned against the fence. I couldn't take Max off, because he was very protective toward me. I was afraid he would bite the Jehovah's witness, if I came near. I had to fetch Jon to come out and call him off.

## Max gone missing

When I came home from work, Max wasn't home. I assumed that William had swung by and taken him for a walk.  Now I am back from the supermarket and Max still is not here.  Max is now diabetic and almost blind, so not up for long walk.  I phone William, and no, he has not been round.  Panic stations. Where is Max?

I grab his lead and hurry to the park across the road.  He is nowhere to be seen.  Not on the footie oval, or the second oval, or anywhere that I can easily see.  Then I realise that I should have thought to change into more sensible shoes for walking in the park.

So I am back in the house, putting on my trainers, when the phone rings.  It is Security, ringing to say that the burglar alarms have gone off in our office.  The office is forty minutes away, in Moorabbin.  I am trying to get Bharat on his mobile, but he is not answering.    Just then, he walks in through the door with Prakash, a friend and colleague, visiting from India.

"That doesn't make sense, we came straight here.  Yes, of course we locked up," they say.

That is a bit more than I can cope with, right now. I am already stressed up about Max.  I can hear a distant rumble of thunder, and Max hates thunder.  Also, it could pour with rain any minute.  I take my car and drive to the next section of the park.  Suppose I don't find him?  He can't see well at all, and he is a bit deaf and arthritic.  He could easily be run over.

This carpark serves the tennis club and the opera shed. I can hear sounds of music and I glance into the shed. There is a rehearsal in progress, and I can dimly see a few people sitting in front of the stage. There is a dark shape lying between them, possibly a school bag. I have a sudden feeling of recognition and look closer. It is Max!

These good people had found him wandering in the carpark in a state of agitation. So they brought him in, for safety's sake. They thought he must belong to someone there. One lady seemed a bit suspicious and walked with us to my car. I wonder what she was thinking.

*There was a simple explanation for the alarms going off. A programmer was still working at his desk. When he stood up to go home, it triggered the alarm. He couldn't remember the code to switch it off, because he had just come back from a three-month break.*

The next day, Max was still a bit shaky, so I took him to the vet. There were a lot of doggy patients, all suffering from anxiety. The vet told me that there had been low-lying distant thunder, several hours before the human ear could detect it, but very disturbing for dogs. He gave Max a dose of Valium and a pack of tablets for the next thunder storm.

I never had to give Max the Valium. He lost his hearing and was never troubled by thunder again.

# The dog beach

The Canadian Bay Club featured in "On the Beach"* with Gregory Peck and Ava Gardner long, long ago.   It is not much changed.  In the movie, Ava Gardner is a local lovely, and Gregory Peck plays the commander of a US nuclear submarine, which has come South to Melbourne to escape an all-embracing cloud of radioactivity.  She has quite a crush on him, but he is still faithful to his wife, even though life on the rest of Earth, has come to an end.

*Watch "Fallout" on YouTube to see more about the making of this Neville Shute movie.

It is a nice place to take young kids for a day on the beach.

Further along, there is a section where dogs are allowed. There is a sign showing where that starts.  Of course, dogs can't read, but the system works well enough.  You wouldn't bother to take your beach gear that far down.   The car park for the dog beach and cliff-walk, is miles away by road because of a gulley.

To go to the dog beach, there is a wooden staircase from the cliff-top and the beach is a bit stony, so you wouldn't choose to swim there.  Plus, because of the gully, the carparks are miles away from each other.

# Bathing with Bella

My grand-dog is a black labrador and she loves swimming. When her Mummy and Daddy go on holiday, she stays with me. This means getting up early for a walk on the beach, because dog-walking ends at 9am, and I don't want to get fined. This is my nearest dog beach, and just a few early risers take their dogs on the beach and have a bit of a chinwag. I put my towel on the sand and chuck my keys on it. Bella has a run with her friends, and I have a bit of a chat. Then I go into the water with Bella. I'm the only one swimming today.

It's nearly nine o'clock, and I am still enjoying the swim. Everyone is leaving and they wave me goodbye. But, oh calamity! When I get out of the water, my keys have vanished. Bella is the most likely culprit, because none of the humans present would do such a thing. Has Bella buried the keys somewhere nearby? No, it seems not. I am scrabbling around in the sand near my towel. Did she run around and drop them somewhere? Or maybe some other dog did it. I am alone, the only person in Canadian Bay, on a chilly autumn day, in wet shorts and t-shirt and I can't get into my car! Furthermore, my phone is inside it. And I am a few miles away from home. All I have is a dog and a beach towel.

To my great relief, I then espied a lady coming round from the Canadian Bay club stairway with a spaniel. I waved at her frantically and waited for her to reach me. Fortunately, she had parked at the dog beach, but been a bit tardy in returning to her car.  After the dogs finally agreed to share the back-seat, she dropped me home.

To make matters even more complicated, I was driving a hire car. They weren't even my keys.  The spare had to be collected from the Hertz head-office in Melbourne.

When I told my daughter about my bad day, she told me off.

"There is a moral to this story, Mum.   Always take a beach-bag.  Do *not* leave your stuff lying around in the open."

## Cheeky Magpies

There are some picnic tables near the Canadian Bay club, with a view over Port Philip Bay.  You can see the sky scrapers in Melbourne, across the water. Distance-wise, it is like looking at France from the white cliffs of Dover.  It is a nice spot to relax and eat some take-away.

I'm dining on chicken and veggies when a magpie lands on my table.  I try to shoo her off. She is rather a surprise because it is usually seagulls which come after your food.

Australian magpies are content to pull worms out of the lawn and sing beautiful songs. But not this one, as it turns out. She thinks she is onto a good thing, bullying picnickers in the park. She is not taking "No" for an answer. On the contrary, she is standing on the table glaring down her big, pointed, black beak at me, with her beady, brown eyes.

Pure aggression. Now, glaring is a trick that seagulls can't do. They have an eye on each side of the face. And their beaks are designed for catching fish in the sea (or French fries in the air). Or for discreetly creeping up behind you and pulling your fish and chips out of a paper bag. A seagull cannot stare you down.

A flock of gulls turns up and they wait hopefully on the grass. They are not too annoying, maybe because I haven't got fish or chips. I look around for the magpie, but I can't see her. Quite suddenly, there is a flap of black wings, and a magpie comes up from under the table and spikes my fried chicken with her beak. Covert action. Actually, a bit creepy. I now see there are a pair of magpies, both looking rather tatty. Probably due to a bad diet and fighting seagulls. A seagull tries to snatch but the magpie is up for it, a morsel of chicken trailing from her beak. I suppose I'm lucky. A seagull would have carried away the whole chicken piece.

Magpies are well known for their aggressive behaviour in the breeding season. They will swoop at your head if you walk, or cycle, near their patch. People can get hurt. I sympathise with the birds. They have the unfortunate task of having to rear their one and only, almost full grown but as yet flightless juvenile, on the ground. A dangerous place to be. A genetic study of magpies revealed that the chick's uncles are the family members given the job of protecting the youngster, while the parents do the feeding.

# Bad hair day?

I had seen the dead bird when I came into work in the morning.  Now I am going home and it is still there. It must've brained itself flying into the new security doors. The doors weren't put there to keep birds out, although at first, I thought they were. The difference between parking outside and under the building is what kind of bird turds you get on your car...

Under the office, pigeon poo.

Outside, seagull shit.

I go for the seagull shit because it's easier escape from there.

But in fact, the gate was installed to keep out people. A prime position beachside shelter for the homeless druggy set. And a great place to charge a phone.  And leave cola cans kicking around the floor.  Possibly do serious damage. Maybe burn the place down by mistake.  Or on purpose.

So there's the bird, lying on its back with its yellow breast feathers showing under its clenched dead feet. A dribble of blood on its head.  I don't want to touch it, but I don't want to leave it there, to get more decomposed every day. I look around and find a stick and a piece of cardboard. I open up a wheelie bin and I'm juggling the bird into the bin, when I notice the people going through bins in the precinct next door. A young man with long curly hair sees me and calls out,

"Lots of good cans in here. But don't bother with the medical ones – you won't get any money for them."

How nice of him to tell me. Just what I needed to know. And I thought I was looking reasonably smart. Am I having a bad hair day? I discretely duck into my Lexus and go home.

## Dog down a hole

I have a reputation for not picking up my feet enough and my balance is not what it used to be. So when I was babysitting and Andy told me not to go out the back-door, because he was digging a hole, I just thought he was worried that I might turn my ankle and fall over.

Andy and Heidi were going to a party. I was already reading a bed-time story to my grand-daughter Billie, when they said goodbye. It was a dress-up, "everybody do an act" affair, so Heidi was wearing a costume, Andy was wearing a funny hat, and they were carrying an amp for Heidi's bass guitar. Off they went, and after a few more stories, Billie and I fell asleep.

I was awakened by a commotion in the house. Anxious voices.

"What's the matter?" I asked.

128

"Tjillyi has fallen in the hole."

"Why didn't she get out?"

"It is six-foot deep.  Andy is down the hole trying to get her out.   I need to help him"

Tjillyi was now an old dog and I had last seen her snoring on her mattress in the playroom.  There is no dog-door so she must have gone out before they left the house – at the bottom of a hole in the rain, patiently waiting.

"If only I had checked!  I'm so sorry.  Poor dog, she has been down there in the rain, all this time,"

"Mum, I am so glad you *didn't* miss her.  Otherwise, you would be in there too!"

## Possums  and Pussy-cats

2022

Australia is famous for its indigenous wildlife, and everybody has heard of the kangaroo and the koala.   But the possum has not achieved fame.  Possibly because it only comes out at night, and lives in trees.

Possums come in different versions.  The "brushtails" are the ones that have truly adapted themselves to urbanisation, and become a bit of a pest. They are the biggest, weighing about 4 kg.   Some of them adapt to city life by snuggling down in a loft and peeing on the ceiling. These city slickers may come to your window, to be fed with chopped apple. Or run around the top of the garden fences, looking for a picnic. Or beg for food at night-time barbecues.

In our garden, we have tiny "sugar gliders" which use a membrane between each hind-foot and front-foot, to glide from tree to tree. Plus we have ring-tailed possums, which are really cute and about the size of a cat. They get their name from their stripey tails.

There are still plenty of trees where we live, so our possums are wild and avoid us. If we have a window open at night, we can hear them calling each other, but we rarely see them. Their call is a hiss with a rattle at the end. A visitor from India got up in a fright, thinking there was a snake under the bed.

Possums are totally nocturnal and completely dazzled in daylight. I found a baby that had fallen from its nest, curled up in a garden bed. It looked a bit like a brown, furry, tennis ball. I disturbed it and it mistook me for a tree. It ran straight at me and up me, really fast. I brushed it off when it got to my face. This happened twice. Then it settled down and grazed a bit on the grass. I went looking for a shoe-box to put it in, but by the time I came back, it had vanished. Hopefully its Mum collected it, when it was dark enough for her to come out of her tree.

We now have a pussy-cat in the family, belonging to Billie and Maleah. Luna is eight months old and completely obsessed with catching anything that moves. She is a silver tabby, very beautiful, with amazing eyes, outlined in nature's mascara. Which brings to mind this verse from The Tiger, by the 18th century English poet, William Blake:

*Tyger! Tyger! burning bright,*
*In the forests of the night:*
*What immortal hand or eye,*
*Dare frame thy fearful symmetry?*

Yesterday, Luna managed to climb a very tall pine tree in the garden. Way out of range of our ladder.

3pm: refused to come down.

5pm: Heidi stood at the very top of the ladder, stretched up and held out her hand. Luna sniffed the hand and then settled on a branch and washed herself.

6pm: (now in darkness) Luna was trying to catch a possum, but it ran onto a thin branch and then jumped into another tree.

Finally tried to come down, got stuck and allowed herself to be helped.

Luna now has a colourful collar, to offset her camouflaged fur. She shot into the house with an angry "noisy miner" clinging to her collar. Luna and the miner birds are now in a state of war. The noisy miner is a honey eater, which also eats seeds and insects.

Luna persists in stalking miner birds in the bottlebrush hedge and the gum trees. The miner birds are smart and work together. They lure her higher and higher into a tree, until the branches are too small to bear her weight. So far, she has had the sense not to fall down. But she did fall in the pool, when she pounced on one and it dodged. Her instincts are driving her to hunt, but when she did catch a bird, she didn't know what to do with it. So we took it from her, undamaged.

The noisy miner is an Australian bird, not to be confused with the "Indian myna", which is an introduced species. The Indian myna is a much-maligned bird, probably because it has taken to urbanisation and annoys city dwellers by shitting on their garden furniture. Any bird (including kookaburras and cockatoos) will shit on garden furniture if it seems like a convenient perch. So it is hardly a capital offence. Yet Brisbane citizens have been encouraged to lure Indian mynas into cages and take them to be euphemised in a gas chamber. Sounds Nazi to me. But then we don't normally have any mynas, where I live. Only one Indian myna visitation ever, which was when a tradie came to remove some tree stumps. A group of five came, to feast on the bugs that turned up in the roots. Now the question is, how did they know he was coming? Do they have spies or something?

# OUR AUSTRALIAN HOME

## A leaky roof story

We should have had our house surveyed before we bought it. We soon found out that the roof was leaky. Unfortunately the house was built when cement tiles were in fashion, and they turned out to be a disaster. It is now well known that cement tiles go brittle with age. Our roof kept springing leaks, which our friendly, neighbourhood plumber patched up with polymer sheeting lined with sawdust.

The climate is a bit iffy though. The first year we were in Melbourne (1982) there was no rain at all. It was a state of drought. This year (2022) it seems to have rained non-stop. Our driveway is a mix of mud and sand and little rivulets of water. Unbelievably, it is still cold as winter and hailing outside, as I sit here writing on November 1st. Much of Victoria is flooded right now.

It took us nearly 20 years to get around to doing something about the leaky roof (largely because we were having very dry weather in those days). We went to a building supplier to choose tiles – real ceramic tiles. But they were completely out of stock – in fact tiles were out of stock everywhere. The Australian taxation system was about to change over to GST, which would make building materials more expensive. So all the builders were stocking up. No shipments expected in the near future.

Of course, nowadays we don't have to wait months for the ship to come in. There is a never-ending stream of goods coming in from China.

We were dismayed at the delay, until Bharat came back from the gym with exciting news. We could have our old roof waterproofed. He had been chatting in the sauna with a guy (we will call him Burp), who claimed he was an expert roof-repairer and had an advertisement in the Yellow Pages. We looked at the ad, and it seemed OK. Even offered a ten-year warranty.

Burp claimed he had spare tiles from a similar roof that he could use to replace our broken ones. He gave us the phone number of an old gent who said he had done a good job. For $10,000 Burp would thoroughly waterproof the roof and put in new gutters. The current ones were leaking like a sieve. In fact, they had holes like a sieve.

At least it was relatively cheap. Retiling the entire roof was a lot of money. Like most Melbourne homes that were built in the days before air-conditioning, our house is single story. So there is a lot of roof.

Actually Burp was a cowboy, and caused us  a lot of sorrow. It all turned out to be a tall story.  I came home from work, to find grey-paint, pussycat pawmarks all along the footpath around the back wall.  Looking up,  I saw a man on the roof, painting in the rain.   Clearly, it was ordinary paint (not silica roof-sealant) because it was running off onto the ground.  I was concerned about the roof, and the health of our cats. I said I needed to speak to Burp but apparently, he was on holiday in Bali.  I told the man to go away.

This is what happened next.

> A tradie came round and power-hosed the roof.  It had stopped raining.  It didn't rain for several months.  So it looked good without the moss.  Little did we know. It was the moss that was keeping the rain out, in most places.
>
> Some tradies replaced the guttering.  It was a bit on the small side, but they did a good job,
>
> Nothing happened for about two months. Burp was still somewhere in Bali. Lucky him.
>
> We were sitting by the pool, when Burp turned up and demanded payment, in full.
>
> *Me: We are waiting for you to repair and seal the roof.*
>
> *Burp: It's all done.*
>
> *Me: No.  Someone came and splashed some grey paint on it.  Look! You can see some splashes on the sun umbrella.  Definitely not waterproofed.*
>
> Burp: OK, I'll fix your umbrella.

Burp walked off with the umbrella and we never saw it again. Or Burp. For a while. Then he invoiced us. For $10,000.

We refused to pay. The next day, he was up a ladder, taking tiles off the roof.

*Me: You can't do that.*

*Burp: Yes I can, they are my tiles.*

*Me: No, none of them are. Stop or I will call the police.*


I went into the house, called the police station, and explained the situation. The policewoman told me to bring Burp to the phone, but he had departed suddenly.


I went to the Legal Aid office, and enquired as to what to do. I said I was happy to pay for the guttering, but no more. They advised to get an architects' report on the roof and file a complaint under Small Claims. And we also had to tell Burp what we were doing.


The inspector came down from the loft and reported that he could see the sky through the roof in several places. It definitely had not been repaired. Armed with his report, we went to the Small Claims Tribunal with confidence. But it had all turned round the wrong way. Burp had filed a counter-claim, asking for his money. The adjudicator had it all back-to-front, and thought we were trying to get out of paying. I said that I was willing to pay $3,000 for the guttering, because that was done.  Anything else that I said, was taken as a feeble excuse for not paying.

It ended up with him being ordered to give us a $1,000 discount, on account of shoddy workmanship. Unbelievable. She insisted on us shaking hands and swearing undying friendship (or something like that). I felt angry.  Really, really churned up inside.  So we had to smile and shake hands, and pay $9,000.

On the way home, Bharat said that I messed up when she asked why we were having the roof sealed, instead of a new roof.  I had replied, "Because of the GST tax".  Apparently, she gave me a disdainful look, as if I were a dirty tax evader.  But then, Bharat could have chipped in and explained the situation - except that he hates confrontation.  That's why I have to be the spokesperson.

## This was not the end of the story

We were still in drought in Melbourne.  Three months later, Bharat and I went to visit cousins for Easter, in Perth WA.  Family members were in our house, having a seaside holiday.   And would you believe, it rained heavily (for the first time since the moss had been taken off) while we were away for Easter.

We had a phone call from Heidi.

"Mum, you will find we have moved the furniture

around a bit. And there is no electricity."

"How come?"

"It rained. It poured. It is still raining. There is water coming through the roof everywhere, so the ceilings are dripping. I've stood your bed on its side against the wall. I've put buckets under all the drips. You will have to call an electrician."

Thank God the house wasn't empty. It was a brand-new king-size bed. I think we would have been in shock if we had come home on the red-eye from Perth and found a flood in the house. (The overnight plane from Perth is known as the red-eye, because you board it at midnight, Perth time, fly for about three hours and land at 6am in the morning, Melbourne time. Only time for a quick nap.

The electrician said that the mouse-bait trays were floating around like boats in our loft, and any mice would have drowned anyway.

Fortunately, a ship with a load of tiles had landed. And would you believe, I got a quote for $10,000 less than the original quote (when the tiles were not available). So we didn't lose much.

Except our peace of mind.

# The burning bird's nest

There was as knock on the door. I opened it, and a very tall Irishman in a yellow builder's vest was standing there.

"You might want to know that there is a bird's nest afire in your lamp-post," he said.


The lamp-post in question is at the top of our driveway, one hundred metres from the house.  A previous owner had the not-so-bright idea of connecting an old-fashioned glass lantern with an ordinary light bulb fitting to the top of the pole (which brings our electricity supply down from the overhead line running down the street). I say not-so-bright because you need a long ladder to change the bulb, and those bulbs don't last long.  Plus there is a risk of electrocution, if you make a wrong move.  Furthermore, there is street light close by, so it is not needed.


The burning bird's nest was my fault. I accidentally flicked the wrong switch, ten minutes before. It must have short-circuited somehow.  I didn't even know that there was bird-nest there.  I hoped that nesting was over, because it was burning spectacularly when I walked up the driveway.


The tenants are rainbow lorikeets, and they still nest every year. The switch is now disconnected.  Birds are very traditional in where they nest. Family members will come back every year, even to the most unsuitable nesting places. My broken lantern is a bit of prime real estate in bird land. I have even been sworn at, by an irate little parrot, when collecting the post!

# Tree through the roof!

Pine trees have a reputation for falling like dominoes and bringing each other down...

On arrival in Australia, our first task was to find a job and a house. The house project was complicated by the fact that we needed a granny flat for my dad. For me, our chosen house was love at first sight. It was well-away from the road and had its own private reserve. A park area full of trees is called a Reserve in Australia, and this garden was definitely full of trees. I am using the past tense, because since a ten-year drought in the 1980s, there are not a lot of trees left.

My experience of trees was limited to the annually lopped plane-trees of the London suburbs, and I thought it wonderful to see trees grow in the way that nature intended. But when the agent was showing us the house, I was a little concerned at the expression on her face when she said, "And here you have our beautiful native trees". She didn't sound quite sincere. We were soon to learn what that was all about.

We had only been in the house for two weeks, when one of the eucalypts uprooted itself. As it was surrounded by other trees, it did not fall far. It merely leant on another one. We were advised to call a 'tree surgeon' to take it down. No harm done. The native trees are prone to falling apart. We had bought into a mix of native Ozzie gum trees and some pine trees left over from a plantation that went bust a century ago, when building bricks suddenly became available in Australia. Pine trees grow quickly and have lots of baby pines. So despite the demise of the plantation industry, our garden had five huge pines quite close to the house.

## Now this is the story of the falling pines

2006

By the time of this event, our children had grown up and left home. I was awoken by a huge CRASH in the middle of the night. As we were not living in one of the world's war zones, the only thing it could be was a falling tree.

I yelled at my husband, "We've got to get up, there is a tree on the house!" He was fast asleep and hadn't heard a thing, but I made him get out of bed.

Our house is single storey and rectangular, with windows down both the long sides. The front door was on a short side, inside the car-port (open garage). We looked out of all the windows, but there was no fallen tree. We were used to the native trees falling down, but they seemed all present and correct. Then we opened the front door and got a big shock. The car-port was criss-crossed with pointed, wooden struts. Rubble and roof tiles, were piled on top of the cars. And, in between the cars, sloping from ground to roof, there was the trunk of a pine tree.

The scariest thing about all this, was that the only thing stopping the tree from crashing onto our bed, was a narrow column of bricks. The fallen tree was exactly in line with the top of the A-frame supporting the roof. The trunk had crashed through the roof and the attic, and stopped when it hit the little brick column. That was pure chance, brought on by the distance of the tree from the house!

## Missed by that much!

All the A-frames over the carport, up to the one over our bedroom wall (just behind our bedhead) had collapsed. The roof supports had easily pierced the plasterboard ceiling and the entire roof above the carport, had fallen through. We could have been skewered by the by the pointed wooden stakes, under a shower of tiles. Plus a tree-trunk, of course. And that was very precariously propped up by the little pillar of bricks. Missed by that much!

We migrated to the granny flat at the other end of the house, and Bharat immediately went back to sleep. I was feeling sick with fear. My first action was to phone the State Emergency Services. They came pretty quickly. After a brief inspection, there was a knock on the back-door.

*"Don't smoke, whatever you do. Your gas main is broken,*

*and we have called the Fire Brigade to deal with it," she said.*

*"Can you remove the tree?" I asked.*

*"No, I am sorry, we can't use our chainsaws with a gas leak. You will have to call your insurance company about removing the tree."*

Of course, I then started freaking out about whether the insurance premiums were up-to-date or not. I couldn't remember how we were paying it. I was desperately going through my accounting folder. No luck! Wherever was it? I couldn't find any recent paperwork. Oh, calamity!

As it turned out, the home insurance was being automatically taken from Bharat's credit card – I needn't have worried. So we phoned the insurance company in the morning.

"Do you need hotel accommodation?"

"No problem," said I, "We are fine staying here."

I was later to regret this decision. As things turned out.

## The morning's events:

Firstly, an official from the town council came around. He served us with a notice to get repairs done ASAP. Including removal of asbestos from the fallen roof. Prompt, but no help at all.

The next visitor was a family of ducks. They had come for a swimming lesson in the pool. They were still in the cute, fluffy stage. Unfortunately, the parents don't understand that the ducklings can't get out again. In a pond, they could walk out. But we humans have built pools that baby ducks cannot escape from. And the parents can't help. All we can do, is try to catch them all, and give them to the mother.

On this occasion, there was still one ducky to go, when Mum decided to walk off with her brood. I ran after her with the babe, but she disappeared under the fallen tree. I let him go, and hopefully they were reunited under the foliage.

*Did you know that immature wood ducks can dive and swim, deep under water, before they can fly? It is no doubt a useful trick for dodging birds of prey, or dogs – but it is a nuisance when you are trying to rescue them from a swimming pool. The best way is to run like mad, and fish them out quickly with the net, when they come up for air. Then the next step is to disentangle their claws from the net. It's best to pop them into a laundry basket until they are all caught. Otherwise Mum can get panicky and leave some behind.*

Just then, the neighbours arrived, and they were also trying to pick their way through the tree branches. They had heard the fire-engine in the night. Right then, an insurance assessor came and went. He took one look and said it wasn't his thing. He only did lean-to car-ports, not carports that were an integral part of a house. Our house looked like a quarter of it had been sliced off with a giant bread-knife.

Some builders came and draped an enormous tarp over the open end of the roof, to protect the loft from the elements. And keep out any possums that might think of taking residence.

Things started to get worse.   Firstly, I noticed that the next-door neighbour's pine tree, which was just the other side of the fence, had developed a slight lean to the left.  The two trees were possibly touching roots.  This was a much heavier tree, which would definitely crush anything it fell upon.  I phoned the insurance company and said I had changed my mind, could we please move into a hotel.   The answer was a firm "No".

My husband and I moved into the spare bedroom at the far end of the house.  Our own bedroom was very noisy when the tarp flapped in the wind. And I was still very scared about the other tree. It was looking more and more unstable. I asked Betty, next-door, if they could do something about it, and her reply was, "Do you expect me to climb up it with a chainsaw?  I'm over eighty."  Of course, I didn't expect that. I phoned a local "tree surgeon" and he said he would have to put in an application to the local council, for permission to take down the tree.  It was too near to a house to take down without a permit.   I thought, it was much too near to three houses not to take down immediately, and there was no knowing which way it would fall, as there was now a strong wind catching its branches.  It was cork-screwing wildly in the wind!  I was scared stiff.

The tree surgeon put in the application, but by the time the council inspector turned up, the tree had a made a spectacular landing. It didn't hit a house. It took ten days to uproot itself, by which time I was a nervous wreck. I was in a meeting at our office when I got a phone call from Betty.

*"Don't come home, Mary!"*

*"What happened?"*

*"The tree fell. But it didn't hit the ground. Don't come down your driveway."*

*Ten minutes later, my friend Christine phoned. I had been staying with her for a few days, to get away from it all. Bharat had gone to India on a business trip. Christine said:*

*"You forgot your pillow. You weren't in, so I dropped it in your carport."*

*'I haven't got a carport anymore,"*

*'Well, I stuffed it into the bar-fridge."*

*"But how did you get down the driveway? I just heard that the tree fell down."*

*"Oh, I didn't see it anywhere. But the neighbours seemed very agitated about something".*

***The funny thing was, that the fallen tree was completely invisible from the driveway if you didn't look up above your head.  Which you don't,  when you are driving a car.***

It was now apparent why the tree had taken so long to fall down.  It had huge roots, and a large tin shed was standing on them.  Except that now the roots were vertical, and the shed was on its side.

Our neighbour Jim, reckoned it must have been the weight of his old text-books that kept the shed in place, but frankly, I don't believe him.  Nobody ever had that many textbooks.  The shed looked pretty heavy, though.

The two pines, supporting the fallen tree,  were only a few metres from our bedroom window.   In stormy weather, the sound of the wind in the pines used to keep me awake at night.  I had always told myself firmly that pines don't fall down, but now I was really alarmed.  They were tall but young and supple, and were bent like bananas, under the weight.   To me, it seemed only a matter of time, before the whole lot fell down.  These trees belonged to another neighbour, and that neighbour had no interest in any of it, because they were a long way from his house. The way home insurance works here, is that it covers the damage done by trees growing on your land. Therefore, we could only claim on the first tree that fell, because that one was ours.  With the others, we were dependent on our neighbours claiming.

Jim put in a claim to have his toppled tree taken down. It took a week or two to go through.  I did a deal with a

147

tree surgeon to take down the two trees supporting it, at a discounted price, if I put his name forward to take down the big one. That organised, he hired an enormous crane (at $10k for a day's hire) to lower each log to the ground. Despite that, one log fell on our steel gatepost and knocked it into the ground like a drawing pin on a notice-board!

I can't remember exactly how many months it took, for all the damage to be repaired. While we were about it, we had the carport converted into a proper garage with walls and doors. This improvement made our bedroom a lot warmer in winter.

## Post script:

I have not told you everything. Some bits were hard to fit in. So I am telling you now.

Firstly, I was not being perfectly accurate, when I said the tree fell between our two cars. Mine wasn't there. We had left it at work, because we were going straight to a friend's house for dinner. So only my husband's car received a shower of rubble, and had to go to the panel beaters. The funny thing is that for him, his car was the main event. Otherwise he was completely unphased. Whilst I was scared stiff, and my blood-pressure went up dramatically.

It turned out that Bharat was telling everybody that a tree had fallen on his Mercedes Benz. Big drama! Without mentioning the house at all. Which explains why I did not receive any commiserating calls from the rellies. In fact, his brothers were quite amazed to find our house completely hidden behind an enormous pile of leafy branches, when they dropped in to see us after all the trees were down. We had spoken on the phone, but I didn't know they didn't know.

The night that the tree fell on our house, we had been to a dinner of left-overs saved from a Jewish religious celebration. Our friends were a Jewish and Muslim couple. To honour the occasion I said grace to all four of our Deities (ours and theirs): Jesus; Krishna; Jehovah and Allah:

"For what we are about to receive, may the four Lords make us truly thankful."

Maybe my prayer was answered.  I leave you to your own opinion on that one.  The tree fell, but we were saved.

# ACCIDENTS

## Accident in Caloundra, Queensland

Caloundra is a seaside town on Queensland's Sunshine Coast. It is best known for its beaches and its cone-shaped "Glass House" mountains. Some friends in California bought a timeshare there, but didn't have time to go to Australia, so we were making use of it for a week. In case you don't remember what a time-share was (as they are no longer popular), you bought some time (at a fixed date) per annum in a holiday resort. Anyway, that was the reason why we were in Caloundra in winter, which is better than Melbourne, but not quite far enough North to swim in the sea. Nevertheless, it was nice and sunny for going for walks.

By the way, the resort pool was also too cold to swim in. Something which is very frustrating about Queensland resorts - the pools don't have heating. Most of the year, they don't need it. What the Queensland tourist industry cannot understand, is that people coming from places that have a real winter, e.g. Melbourne or Scotland, are looking forward to swimming in the sunshine. But the sunshine is useless when the nights are cold and consequently the pool is too. No wonder everybody goes to Bali instead.

Anyway, this story is about a car accident and all its ramifications. My plan was, to make use of the trip (distance from Melbourne) to sell our e-learning programs to local schools. I had made an appointment with a local Christian school, and Bharat dropped me there. He is a badminton fanatic, and had arranged to play at a local club. So off he went.

I had a nice chat with the school's science coordinator, and all went well. He agreed to buy a system for year 11 and 12 and some individuals who needed special help. I sat down to wait for Bharat in the school lobby, and I waited and waited. I am a teacher, not a salesperson, and I felt quite embarrassed. Then a complete stranger came to pick me up. I was quite alarmed when she told me that Bharat had had an accident, but she assured me that he was quite OK, just delayed at the scene.

Well, this is the story. Bharat was driving through a residential area, taking a short cut on the map, when someone backed out of a driveway without looking. Bharat took evasive action, and hit a car parked on the other side of the road. You wouldn't think that an accident like that would result in serious injury, but it did.

The lady who owned the parked car, heard the crash and looked out of the window. To her horror, she saw her car all smashed up, and promptly fell down the stairs. Consequently, the police and an ambulance had to attend. Hence the delay. I do hope she wasn't badly hurt, but we never got to hear about it. All I know is, that she was carried out on a stretcher, poor woman.

In Queensland, the police can make a ruling on the spot. This is very convenient, especially if it goes your way.  No uncertainty, or arguments between insurance companies. Their ruling was that the neighbour who reversed, was responsible for it all.  Also, the police called a repair man, who towed the car back to his shop.  This turned out not to be so good, because he tried to hang on to the car, no matter what.  He insisted that it would take two weeks to get the spares and get the job done, and we just didn't know what to do.  We were due to go home in 4 days.  Our insurance company wasn't helpful.

Fortunately, I had the idea of phoning the RACV.  They said, "Didn't your insurance company offer to transport your car home?  Then you can choose your repairer at your leisure." Well, nobody had told us that, and we had been fretting for nothing.  However, nearly two thousand kilometres in a bus is a bit much.  It could have been a bit easier, but at such short notice, the first lap had to be a local bus to Toowoomba. Unfortunately, we were sitting behind a mum with a baby on her lap, and he was having a very smelly attack of diarrhea. All the way there. Very, very pongy.

The journey from Toowoomba to Melbourne wasn't too bad, just rather uncomfortable.  This bus had a toilet, and the driver repeatedly announced that anyone who used it for a poo, would be thrown off the bus. There were regular loo and sandwich stops, so we survived.

The car was safely delivered and repaired locally in Melbourne.

## Why do I find such weird ways to injure myself?

I broke my right shoulder catching my slipper in a mat between two sofas. Three months later, I broke my left arm trying to switch on the pool pump. Six years later, I broke my right wrist when visiting a friend in aged care. And now guess what I did! I slipped a disk trying on pyjamas in a fitting room.

As my physiotherapist said this morning, they are very nice pyjamas. (His receptionist gave me ten minutes notice to grab a cancellation. I just didn't have time to struggle into my clothes. So I turned up in pink pyjamas with lots of little pandas on them).

How did I do it? Main Street Mornington is my favourite shopping ground. I have been looking for pyjamas for a while, and I went to a Myer sale on Friday, and found nothing interesting. So when I saw a rail full of fluffy, pastel-coloured pyjamas with baby pandas, displayed outside a boutique, I just had to go into the shop and try them on.

Unfortunately for me, the fitting rooms were rather unusual. They were more like tents. All four walls were made of a purple, flowery fabric. No bench, no chair. A painted concrete floor. Two picture hooks on the rail, to hang the wooden hangers.

I should have asked for a chair. But no, I didn't. I have often remarked that, to survive the passing years, it is essential not to balance on one leg to put your knickers on. That is potentially suicidal. So I grabbed onto one of the corner poles, tastefully covered in the purple, flowery fabric. Then I tried to put my leg through the trouser leg on the pyjamas. My right hand was up and my spine was twisting while I tried get my left leg into the trouser leg. Effectively I was doing a golf swing. So it is hardly surprising that I slipped a disk! I felt it clunk then, but the pain didn't kick in until the evening.

Fortunately, my physio was able to slip it back into place when he opened on Monday. Not so much of a disaster, after all. Just a weekend full of pain.

Getting back to the pool pump (when I broke my left wrist), it was January in Melbourne 2012 and a cold morning in a really pathetic summer. I had broken my right arm at the shoulder, and the muscles and tendons just weren't letting go. It was as if my elbow was glued to my side. The hospital physio recommended exercising in the pool. But the pool was cold and the pump was off, so I couldn't put on the heater. I had asked for all the pool things with poles to be put out of the way, because I couldn't do it one-handed.

Some bright spark had decided to tie them horizontally to the filter. I couldn't reach over to switch on. I managed to untie the knots holding one end of the poles together. And I dropped that end of the poles on the ground, the other end still being tied up.

I stepped over the poles, switched on the pump, and then stepped backwards. Big mistake! You know the movie scene where the person being chased, sets some round things rolling down and the pursuer goes flying? Well that is what happened to me. I stood on the poles and threw myself backwards, smashing the back of my wrist on the ground. Producing a nasty compound fracture.

Being January, and everyone short-staffed, by the time it was operated on the bones had knitted incorrectly. The young surgeon who operated on me, told me that he had had to cut through them all to reset. That also involved cutting through the nerves. He said my wrist bones looked like a violet crumble bar. I had to retrain my fingers by posting counters into a Connect Four game (you have to make a row of four).

The following week, I had an appointment with an osteoporosis specialist. This was a follow-up on my broken shoulder, three months earlier. I had been sent for a scan to check on the condition of my bones. I went into his room at the hospital, with one arm in plaster in a sling, and the other only moveable from the elbow down. Not looking up from his paperwork, he commented, "The scan showed that your bones are good. You would have to fall down a cliff to break anything,"

I replied, "Look at me!"

# Bursting with Goodness:

I can't drink wine, because I'm allergic, and I am not terribly fond of beer. But sometimes, just sometimes, I fancy a glass of beer with my evening meal. I have family staying in the granny flat (where the bar fridge is) and I know Andy bought me a half-dozen Light Ale, but I can't remember where I put them. I look in my fridge, and there isn't any. Next, I open the pantry, and to my surprise, there is a big puddle on the floor. Where did that come from, suddenly? It is pouring with rain, but the ceiling is dry, and the puddle doesn't reach the walls. Now this is a puzzle. It doesn't seem to come from anywhere.

I start checking the pantry shelves. The bottom one is sticky. The one above is sticky. I dip my fingertip in the water on the floor, and sniff it. It smells of apple-juice. But it is wet, not sticky. I had to move some saucepans, but it looks like it came from the left, back corner.

I stand on a stool and start taking things off the shelves. Some things are wet, some are sticky. A red and yellow box of Lipton's English Breakfast teabags is sticky on top, but perfectly dry within. Well done Lipton's! I don't drink black tea myself, it's for friends.

As I work my way up the shelves, I find a few things that are sopping wet. A floppy, saturated packet of spaghetti. Ah, this might be the culprit! A soggy cough syrup box. But no, the bottle is perfectly intact.

I am wearing kitchen gloves and wiping up as I go, throwing the wet or sticky stuff in a binbag. I don't know what I am handling, so I am being careful. Now here is a mystery: a 1.5 L glass storage jar with an airtight glass lid (containing some sandwich bags of herbal teabags, that I have forgotten about) has some yellow liquid inside. I will have to run an experiment on that.

I am now at the top-shelf and, straight above the storage jar, I have found the culprit. It is a tall can of pear juice. I pick it up, and it is light as a feather. Perfectly intact, but empty. I am trying to find the leak. I shake it. It rattles, but not a drop comes out. All gone. Closer inspection finds a little black mark on the label, near the bottom of the can.

A friend bought the juice for me, years ago. Now, I am a bit nervous of "fresh" juice from local producers. There was a recall on TV, some time ago. Nasty food-poisoning. But unfortunately, I am no good at throwing things away. But I do have some gremlins, which move things I don't use, to the back of the fridge. There, they take on the look of a scientific experiment, until I find them moldering. One of those gremlins must have got loose in my pantry, and moved the can out of my line of vision.

I am really worried. It is possible that my pantry is now contaminated with botulism. Botulism is incredibly toxic, just tasting it can be lethal. That's all I need! Glad I only sniffed. I look up botulism on the internet: "A rare but serious bacterial infection caused by Clostridium botulinum." Botulism is a toxin given out by anaerobic (no air) bacteria that can grow in cans or bottles that are not industrially processed. Fruits or veggies, with low acidity, are at risk. It can be discoloured, smelly, or taste bad, or there may be no sign at all. I quickly put the can in the bin and wash my hands.

I don't know when it reached its USE BY DATE, but it has definitely reached its EXPLODE BY DATE.

Next day: What is really freaking me out, is that any of the juice anywhere, could be highly toxic. And it seems to have spattered all over the pantry. I have done an experiment with the glass storage jar. After cleaning it, I put the airtight lid on firmly and stand it in the sink, under the tap. The water flowed all over the outside, while it slowly filled up on the inside. The water clings to the glass (through surface tension) and somehow gets under the lid. Which means I cannot trust anything that has been sprayed by the pear juice. Better to be safe than sorry. Time for a massive throw out.

I take the can out of the bin – by now the paper label is darkening all over – and look for the USE BY DATE. There isn't one, only a serial number. But guess what – the slogan on the label is:

## ALL NATURAL AUSTRALIAN PEAR JUICE – BURSTING WITH GOODNESS

So that's what happened!

# WINTER HOLIDAYS IN THE SUN

## Mossman Gorge...Help!

One of the great things about Australia is, that you can pick your climate. We were enduring a very cold July in Melbourne, and when I asked Heidi if she fancied a holiday in Tropical North Queensland, she gave an enthusiastic "Yes". Her hubby was working in the US, at a huge "Eclipse of the Sun" Festival, so she had no ties. We found a house to let near Daintree on beautiful Cape Tribulation.

*Cape Tribulation was named by Captain James Cook, because that was "where all his tribulations began". Think about it, he had sailed from England, rounded Cape Horn, visited Tahiti and sailed completely around New Zealand. Would you believe his tribulations didn't start until then, after being almost two years at sea? Unfortunately, after they started, they never seemed to stop. The Endeavour went aground on the Great Barrier Reef, and was so badly damaged, that after miraculously patching her up, they had to leave Australia and head for the nearest shipyard. In what we now call Jakarta, Indonesia.*

The Mossman River flows through a crack in the Great Dividing Range, at the edge of the Daintree rain forest. The river has amazing granite boulders, polished by the fast-flowing waters, until they are completely smooth and rounded. The flow is unpredictable because, even when there is no sign of rain, the mountain peaks can skim water from passing rainclouds. Therefore, swimming in the river is not advised. But the Mossman Water Hole is said to be a safe place to swim and a beauty spot attracting holiday makers from nearby Port Douglas, or on a road trip up the coast through the Daintree and Cape Tribulation.

I was with Heidi and her daughters, Billie and baby Marleah. We had to park the car in the carpark, buy an entry ticket and take a short bus trip down to the water hole. There was a "Local Conditions" board in the carpark, with the arrow pointing to "No swimming today". Everyone at the stop was puzzled. It seemed a perfect day. How come they are selling tickets? And so on.

The bus has come, and we have arrived at this beautiful water-hole in the bush, and put down a tarp to establish our position. It all looks so serene. People are swimming peacefully. There is not a ripple on the water. Billie (she can swim OK) is paddling. I am floating on my back and idly chatting with a young African woman from London.

*Quite suddenly, I feel myself being jet-propelled, head first, toward the rocks. I try to swim but I can't do anything. So I scream for help. I already have boulders on either side of me. Another swimmer grabs at my fingers but I can't hold on. I am shouting at him to hold my wrist. He does. He is clearly not experienced at this kind of thing. After all, who is? He has his feet on the ground, which is an advantage. He helps me to climb on to a rock. But I am faced with a great big boulder.*

*Meanwhile, Heidi has thrust the baby into a complete stranger's arms, with a cry of "That's my Mum down there!" and made her way down to the rocks. She tells my saviour firmly, "I can take it from here," and pulls me up the boulder. I could have done with a bum-lift, but never mind. Two more boulders to go.*

*When we reach the top, I realise that I have an audience. Everyone is watching. My newfound friend from London calls out,*

*"Come back down, I'll look after you!"*

*"I think I have caused enough trouble already," I reply.*

I am just thankful that it was me who got dragged away, and not Billie. Heidi is telling me off for floating in a waterhole. She says that being pulled down a cascade is always a risk. Now you tell me!

I have since googled this tourist info:

## Swimming at Mossman Gorge

*Mossman Gorge features a sheltered swimming hole where the pristine rainforest water flows around spectacular granite boulders, and a sandy beach forms a perfect entry point into the water. Anyone planning on swimming should exercise caution and observe local conditions before entering the water. Swimming is not recommended for inexperienced swimmers, the elderly or small children.*

## Whale watching at Ningaloo Reef

This is another serendipity story. Not long after we moved from England to Melbourne, I had a call from Jay Spencer, editor of the computer section of The Age, asking me to do a user-story on a brand-new concept: word processing. Now that *is* something that has caught on in a big way! Jay didn't have a budget for freelances, but the computer manufacturer, Wang Inc, was happy to pay. So off I went to the Ford Factory in Broadmeadows, to see word-processing in action.

There was I, in the engineering office, when who should I see, but an old friend from my Atomic Energy Authority days. We had kept up for a few years, but then lost touch. Could it be Brian? He didn't look any older and I hadn't seen him for about fifteen years. I walked up to his desk, and sure enough, he had a long nameplate on his disk. Labelled.

*"Hallo Brian," said I.*

*"Hallo, Mary," said Brian, "Are you married?"*

*"Yes, with three children," said I.*

*"That is very married," said Brian.*

Those niceties dealt with, we exchanged telephone numbers and arranged to organise a family get-together.

I had no idea Brian had migrated to Australia.    It was a chance meeting, and I am so glad of it, because his wife and I have become great friends.  We  both started our careers with the UK Atomic Energy Authority and later became Maths teachers on starting a family.  And we do have a good laugh together!  We can be truly silly.

Brian and Helen did not stay very long in Melbourne, but eventually settled in Perth, Western Australia (more than three hours flight and a lot of dollars away from Melbourne). Nowadays, Helen is a widow, and I am single, but we manage to get together for holidays.

In 2018 we got together for a sunshine holiday in Northern WA, during the Melbourne and Perth winter.  Exmouth is on the Ningaloo reef, known for migration of humpback whales and whale sharks. I had come across humpback whales often enough on the East Coast, but whale sharks are another story.  They are huge, up to 18 metres long, but they won't eat you, as they are filter feeders.  It would be amazing to see them, they are actually dark blue with white spots on but, in order to see them, you have to swim in the water above them, so not our cup of tea. None but the brave. We chose the humpback excursion.

The boat we went out on was a family business and well established. But it was a bit of a rough day. We were both keen on taking photographs of the humpback whales jumping out of the water. It is a great sight to see. Humpbacks are huge. As big as the boat. And they came right up close. But major problem, the boat was rocking a lot. So we focused our cameras on the leaping whale as soon as it appeared, and then it disappeared from our viewfinders. We managed to photograph their tails flapping, but the body roll is much harder to catch.

I remember a Patrick Swayze movie, where he is asked why humpbacks leap out of the sea. His answer (from the script):

"Because they can!"

I like that. But maybe David Attenborough would have a better answer.

We had chosen to sit on the top deck in order to get a good view and be able to take photos. As there is no knowing which side of the boat they are going to appear on, we chose to sit on the bench in the middle (where they keep the lifebelts and stuff). Unfortunately the further we went out to sea, the more the boat rocked and swayed. The other tourists were gradually disappearing below deck, but when we tried to stand up, we had to sit down again suddenly. There was nothing to hold on to, except each other. Oh, and the unopened bottle of red wine that Helen was clinging to!

We were trying to get up,  giggling and feeling complete idiots, but there was no escape. At last a crew member came up on deck and saved us.

*"You are brave to stay up here!  Come and have some food."*

*"Help us please!  We can't stand up."*

So she grabbed us both by the arm and somehow managed to steer us toward the steps, where we grabbed the handrail and staggered down to the deck below.   Just as well or we would have missed out on the amazing Exmouth prawns which were being served up with the salad.   On the first round we daintily took just one prawn each, thinking that was our share.   But the prawn plate kept being refilled. Huge, beautiful prawns.  Imagine what that would cost in a restaurant!   We did have a second helping but we're not greedy.

A nice lady came and had a chat with us. And then she asked us a question:

*Are you two married?*

*"No," said I, "I'm divorced, and my friend is a widow."*

And then it dawned on me. Same sex marriage was much in the news. There had just been a referendum about it. She must have mistaken lack of mobility for passion. She thought we were two giggly lovers on our honeymoon. Probably her friends had asked her to find out.

Personally, I didn't fill in the referendum papers, because same sex marriage was already legal anyway, so there was no real point. Also, I found the wording concerning. The writers were bending backwards to be politically correct. The result being that there was no mention of homosexuality or lesbianism. Now I understand that would be hard to prove, from a legal point of view. But couldn't the referendum simply state that no statement of gender is required? Instead of promoting same sex marriage as an option for everybody. Puberty and growing up is confusing enough already, without any more choices.

## Airlie Beach – a secret destination?

The sun is setting gently behind the mountains, a soft shade of pink. Soft as the summer air. The sea, like a clear grey mirror perfectly reflecting the little white boats at their moorings. Soon the cockatoos will come to their roosts, swooping and squawking as they land secretly at nightfall – just as they take off at the first glimmer of sunrise, in the safety of darkness.

All this sea and sun, and yet little known. One of the world's best kept secrets. A cruise ship lies at anchor offshore, bringing visitors from Brisbane, Sydney and Melbourne.

Maybe this will put Airlie Beach on the map. The amazingly beautiful Whitsundays are hardly known to Australian holiday makers, although Airlie is very popular destination for European backpackers. Now let's think about this. Why could this be? Why don't Victorians go further North than Noosa? You might call that a failure of the Queensland tourist industry.

When we migrated to Australia from England, I was amazed that so many Victorians had never been to Sydney. Of course, the distance is huge, but still! Wouldn't you want to see? However, Queensland's Gold Coast was well-developed as a holiday escape, and Surfers Paradise was the place to go for a September family holiday.

So we went to Surfers Paradise with the kids, I stepped into the sea, my feet were promptly pulled from under me, and a wave crashed over my head. Not my cup of tea. But later, much later, we discovered the Whitsundays and further north, the Daintree National Park. And I fell in love with beautiful and unspoilt Australia, and wished that we had explored more before.

Unfortunately for Queensland tourism, just when entrepreneurs were enthusiastically starting to develop holiday destinations for Australians in Australia, the whole scenario changed and Australians started to go overseas. International tourism became a huge industry, with not a lot of it incoming to Australia. On the contrary, putting senior citizens into cruise ships or packing us off to see the wonders of the world, was the travel agency's bread-and-butter until COVID-19. Even during the pandemic, the focus was on booking us into cruises on some unknown future date.

I would very much like to see our travel agents enticing us to holidays in Australia. It will require some effort. And organised discount travel.

For decades, it was cheaper to fly to Bali. And a lot cheaper when you got there. The Australian dollar goes a long way in Bali. Bali was the place to go with your mates and party with other Aussies. So after the Bali bombing, the papers were full of "What can we do to restore our Bali?" Of course it's not our Bali – Bali belongs to Indonesia. And it's too hot and humid for me. Here, we have a place of stunning natural beauty, with sheltered sailing and resort accommodation, and it's at home – in Australia. It's not an Asian country! It's not prone to terrorism or executing tourists for drug offences.

I love sailing, which is why the Whitsundays appeal to me. Of course, you can drive all the way up there, but that is 2,500 kilometres from Melbourne. Thirty hours continuous driving! Or you can take a real break and do a road-trip for a few months. Lots of people do.

At the present date (2022) there are direct flights from Melbourne or Sydney to Proserpine, which is the airport for Airlie. I would like to point out that, because of the huge distances involved, in Australia, planes take a long time to get to their destination and come back again. So "a few flights" can mean five in a week. You need to book well in advance. And you need to book carefully too. Flight websites have an annoying way of picking up roundabout routes which take all day, and involve changing planes, with airport landing fees at each airport upping the price to something quite unreasonable. You would have to be desperate. Very important to take a direct flight, or read the time-table very carefully. Otherwise, you may be arriving the day after.

## Amazing News

November 2022

*Virgin has just opened up direct flights between Brisbane and Los Angeles! An eight thousand US dollar return fare in economy. Seventeen hours flight. This could be a big boost for Queensland tourism, if handled well.*

## Spirit of Queensland

2019

It is easy to overlook the fact that Queensland has nearly 7 thousand km of mainland coastline, plus another 6 thousand km of island coastline. Furthermore, the mainland runs from South to North. But although it can offer spectacular scenery, perfect holiday playgrounds in sun and sea, and an escape from winter, tourism is hampered by most coastal towns being thousands of miles from anywhere. Anywhere else in the world, anywhere else in Australia, or indeed, anywhere else in Queensland.

The Spirit of Queensland is a modern tilt train that runs the length of the Queensland coast between Brisbane and Cairns. The train makes the 1,681km journey five times per week and takes 25 hours. In other words, a night and a day. There are many stations on the way, so you could plan a holiday involving stayovers in various coastal towns. I had a bit of a google and here is some interesting information on travel times:

Plane: 3 hours 54 minutes.

Train: 24 hours 45 minutes.

Car (continuous driving): 21 hours 24 minutes

Bus: 29 hours 25 minutes. I would hate to do that one.

I am not quoting prices, because those vary a lot. For trains, there are special offers for seniors, pensioners, students etc.

The fly-in-the-ointment with the train journey, is that many of the stations involve boarding or leaving the train in the middle of the night! It is always the same time for any given place. For example, if you live in Bundaberg, you probably won't use it, because it passes through Bundaberg at 3:30am.

My particular problem, is catching it in Proserpine at 6:30am. We have a holiday unit at Airlie Beach, Whitsundays, and Proserpine is the nearest station, a twenty-minute drive. My destination is Townsville, a three-and-a-half-hour journey. From there, I must take a short boat trip to Magnetic Island, where I am getting together with my friend Helen, who is flying out from Perth. The only way to get to the station at this early hour, is in a taxi. I need to leave at 5:40am, latest. My worry is that, even if I organise everything properly, it can go all wrong, because hotel reception doesn't open until 8am. If the taxi goes to reception, instead of up the hill to the unit, I have no way of getting there with my bags.

Today, all went well. A very helpful taxi-driver picked me up and carried my bags to the platform for me. I had one wheely suitcase and a big, throw-away zip bag for the purchases I had made.

I had flown up to Airlie, from Melbourne, two weeks earlier with my friend Diane. She went back the day before I left, because I wanted to see her safely on to the plane. We hit some problems at the airport. Diane was relying on taking some cash from the airport ATM. It wasn't there. I didn't have any cash on me either. This is a small airport with just one gate – you can't really lose an ATM. Someone said it had been moved. We were rushing round in circles looking for it, but it definitely wasn't there. Then someone else told us it had been taken away for servicing. By that time, the passengers were already being called.

Diane was the last through the gate. Ping, ping! From the metal detector. Now Diane loves her rings and her bling. She is festooned with it. Encouraged by airport security, she is taking off one bit at a time. No luck. Ping, ping again.

Airport security suggests her cigarettes. The metal wrapper can ping.

No Luck.

I am thinking about this, and the only thing Diane is wearing, that she wasn't wearing on arrival, is the pair of earrings she purchased at Airlie Market. They are sparkly and Security thinks it is unlikely to be them. Diane carefully unscrews them from her ears, with dramatic gestures.

Hooray! Those sparklers were made of foil. She's through and none too soon. They are having the last call at the gate.

## On the train

You might want to know why I have chosen to take a three-hour train journey to Townsville instead of flying. Well, the thing is this. To fly from one town to another along the Queensland coast, the only way is to change planes at Brisbane. So, to travel along the coast from town to town by plane, you must go up and down the coast, like a yoyo.

The station master is putting tags on my suitcase and asks for my ticket. He needs to know what carriage I am going in. I show him the printout I have from the internet.

"That's not a ticket! You need a seat reservation"

"Oh!"

"It's OK, I can print you a ticket at the ticket office."

And he does, but the train is at the platform, and I am panicking.

Another railway person is herding people onto the train. She wants to know which carriage I am in, but I don't know what I have done with my ticket. I have only had it for two minutes and I've already lost it.

"Don't worry, just get in, calm down and find your ticket, and walk down the train.   Your luggage is already there."

Grand idea.   And interesting. I find my ticket and I am in Carriage F.   Some carriages have daytime passengers like myself. Others have the blinds closed and people sleeping. They must have got on yesterday.   I think the next one is mine.   This is a darkened carriage, and it smells of vomit. Oh, thank God this is "G". I've gone too far! I turn round and go back into F, which is bright and airy, and I have a comfy seat by myself.

In all fairness, the Spirit of Queensland does have some luxury berths for sleeping on the train.   At a price.   My seat is like a good plane seat, with a choice of on-flight entertainment and a scenic window from floor to ceiling. There is a little café in the next carriage.

It is not the first time I have travelled on the Spirit of Queensland.   I once took the ten-hour train journey from

Proserpine to Cairns. It was the end of "Schoolies Week", which means that loads of teenagers were returning to Victoria after wild times on the Gold Coast - a rite of passage on finishing school forever. All the planes going South were booked up, but Cairns had direct flights to Melbourne, and they were only $200 dollars. Not bad for a three thousand km journey. Even though Cairns is entirely in the opposite direction – going North - it was the only way to get to Melbourne. And while I was there, I did some sight-seeing in Cairns and its hinterland.

Although the train was nice enough, I would hardly call it a scenic route. I was expecting coastal views, but we were always a bit inland. I took some pics, but they all looked the same. A bit of greenery on one side and some small mountains on the other. Plus an occasional dumping ground for old Holden cars. The actual coastline is very wiggly and neither the highway, nor the railway, travel along it.

# MAGNETIC ISLAND AND A FISHY STORY

Magnetic Island is great lump of granite, thrown up out of the sea, and rising to 497 metres at its highest point. Captain Cook thought it was magnetic because his ship's compass kept taking him there. Maybe it was just an ocean current. The huge black boulders, some as high as a cathedral, are definitely granite, and not magnetic.

The community was founded in 1898, by Robert Hayles, an adventurous entrepreneur from Townsville. He opened a pub in Picnic Bay, with a jetty and a boat service for day-trippers from the mainland. The pub is still going strong, although the original building is long gone, as a result of fire and cyclones.

I find Magnetic Island quite charming in that it is remarkably unspoilt. You feel that it is loved by all its inhabitants - koalas, rock wallabies, birds, corals, insects, golden butterfly fish and humans. One thousand, one hundred and twenty-six species all together, according to a citizen science survey!

177

Not bad for an island covering only twenty square miles! See *inaturalist.org*

The first morning I awoke very early, to the sound of some raucous birds I didn't recognise. I strolled down to Picnic Bay and found it very, very busy. It was the day of the annual swimming race to Townsville. Wow, I didn't expect that. It was all very organised, with a canoe accompanying each swimmer. It was a very colourful show on the beach – each team had its own jersey. The distance between Picnic Bay and Townsville is about eight km.

## Painting

Helen had the bright idea of painting the scenery while we were there. She was arriving a few days after me, so I thought it would be a good idea to do some painting to pass the time. I packed my art stuff into the little car and followed the coast road, looking out for a suitable site to capture the amazing granite formations. The difficulty was to find a comfortable place to sit, with a clear view. I was drawing in pastel, and I found as I drew, that the colour and shape of the rocks was changing with the sunlight. Not only did they vary from black to pink, but the shapes seemed to change as well. It was as if the thing I just painted was replaced with a different rock! A trick of the light on the uneven and multicoloured surface of granite.

The following morning, when I was standing at my kitchen sink, I happened to look upwards, out of the kitchen window. To my surprise, I saw a beautiful heap of granite boulders, high above me, glowing pink in the early morning light. I could have painted them in comfort. And so I did, sitting at a table in the garden. First, I went for an exploratory walk, and found myself standing on the horizontal foot of a great granite wall which terminated in the spectacular boulder formation high, high above.

# A bit of trouble on Horseshoe Bay Road

The only road to join the holiday attractions of Picnic Bay, Nelly Bay and Horseshoe Bay was built with picks and shovels by workers In 1920. It has a cliff on one side and a sheer drop on the other, and it is only 20km long. Despite this, there are 3 car hire firms, competing for custom, mainly from day trippers, coming over on the ferry from Townsville. I had hired a very small and somewhat worn-out vehicle. It tended to go slightly out of control on the downhill bits, and I couldn't see a thing at night. The last ferry leaves before sunset, so working headlights were not a priority for day trippers!

Helen and I had booked a sunset cruise from Horseshoe Bay. Unfortunately, both of us were waiting for cataract operations and couldn't see very well at night. The problem with that was, that when you disembark from a sunset cruise, the sun has definitely set. So how were we going to drive home in the dark? The only solution was to swap the car for something better. Which we managed to do, after waiting around all morning for a suitable car to come in. This was a decent hire-car, with working head lights.

We had a beautiful cruise under sail, round the north-western coast. All the beaches are on private land, with a backdrop of National Park, so it is unspoilt and abounding with bird-life. Our hosts (mother and son) lived onboard their boat, and served us mocktails and nibbles. As we came home into Horseshoe Bay, we were moving almost silently in the twilight, amongst the shadowy forms of the other yachts. There was a feeling of stillness and a golden glow on the horizon. By the time we picked up the mooring on Horseshoe Bay, the sun was already disappearing over the horizon, and it was dark as we climbed down the side of the boat, into the tender.

Remember, we were concerned about keeping on the road in the dark! I was driving, and the wiggly mountain road was clearly defined by red reflectors. Not so bad! But when we were out of that and driving on the flat, breathing a sigh of relief, I noticed that everyone behind me was turning right. How come?

Oh calamity, we are on the beach!

Fortunately, the sand was solid and we could reverse back on to the road.

# The Brahminy Kite

(White-bellied Sea Eagle)

Helen and I booked a Magnetic  Island discovery tour in Aquascene, a flat-bottomed boat.  It was a sightsee and snorkel tour with a bit of fishing thrown in.  Our skipper was a local.  He had grown up there, seen the world and then come back again.   He sat down beside us and handed me a small fish.

"Hold it up. Raise your arm.  That's right, keep it there,' said he, taking out his phone to take a photo.

Everyone is looking.  I am asking myself, "Why am I  sitting here, holding a fish up in the air?"

Then I notice an eagle winging its way toward me.  Suddenly, it comes straight at me, grabs the fish in its talons and flies away with it.

I am in shock.  I hear myself shout out, "Bloody Hell!"  Laughter all round.

The skipper has recorded it all in slow-mo, on his phone.  He plays it back to us.  You should see the look of horror and astonishment on my face!   In slow-mo!

I put the clip on my Facebook page.  Fortunately, as it was in slo-mo, none of my friends watched long enough to hear me swear.

181

*The fish-snatch looks impressive though. It just goes to show what a wild bird can be trained to put into its morning routine!*

## A summer holiday in England

2004

England seems much prettier than I remember it. As we drive through the narrow country lanes, almost every village dwelling is adorned with hanging baskets of busy Lizzie and bright red geraniums; as if bursting out with colour, just to please the passer-by.

Cottages are freshly painted and newly thatched, hedges are perfectly clipped, and picturesque inn-signs hang jauntily from the village pubs; just as it must have been, when they first opened in some period of prosperity many centuries ago. In fact, wherever we roam: Yorkshire, the Midlands, the Welsh border or the Fens, the countryside is just posing for a photograph of Quaint Olde England.

I was beginning to think that my memories of rotting wooden beams and blackened, leaking thatched roofs, and hedges which reached out to meet each other across the roads, must have been the inaccurate observations of a youthful Londoner, when my cousin Bill in Bristol threw some light on the matter.

"The countryside is now owned by rich people with gardeners. Executives are moving out of London and paying a hundred pounds a week (more than $A250) to commute from Bristol to London on the train. House prices have gone up enormously. All the way to London is nothing nowadays."

For one reason or another, England appears to have shrunk. Now I expected everything to seem small when coming from a big country like Australia. But there is more to it than that. While we were away, really good motorways have been built — which can sweep you into London at remarkable speed if you are lucky. And of course, if you feel inclined, you can actually drive right into France (on a train through the Chunnel) for a day-trip.

By chance, when visiting friends in Harrogate, I started reading a book by George Orwell (author of Animal Farm) where he reported on the miserable conditions of life in the slums of the industrial north, a century ago.  North country bars used to be 'spit and sawdust' and girls weren't allowed. The dull old brewers' house signs have now come down and been replaced by a neatly painted "The Pig and Whistle" or "Horse and Hounds". Public Bars are being refurbished as classy restaurants or bistros and are doing splendidly.

Of course, there is a downside to all this. Heavy industry has almost completely disappeared. Modern industries, less damaging to the environment, come and then go away again. For example, a well-known International opened a plant in Tyneside, which lead to a council-housing estate being built around it. But after a couple of months the plant closed down on the grounds of over-production somewhere. It probably opened up again in some other country with some other government's support. But this kind of thing leaves the locals confused and worried and as convinced as ever that the government in the South doesn't really care and never ever will.

# THE PANDEMIC AND OTHER DISASTERS

## New Year's Day

2020 began badly and got steadily worse. On New Year's Day, I woke up in the morning, and tried to get out of bed. Before my feet touched the ground, an unseen hand threw me backwards, flat on my back on the bed. I tried to get up three times, all with the same result. It was very scary.

I wondered if I was having a stroke. I immediately phoned my son Jonathan, asking him to take me to hospital ASAP. He is only a five-minute drive from me. While he was on his way over, I tried carefully sitting up and putting my head between my knees. That calmed me down and I was able to stand, but I still felt very unsteady.

Now, you probably think that I overdid the New Year's Eve celebrations – but I had only been to the local cinema with some friends. It was a good movie – I wish I could remember what it was. When it finished, I tried to stand up to go up, but I found myself losing my balance. My friends were chatting excitedly about the movie – while I was groping my way out. I didn't mention anything. Someone said, "Can you give Beth a lift, you are going her way." My car was parked right in front of the cinema, and I got in and drove Beth home successfully, but when I got home, I could barely stagger into the house and fall on my bed. The next thing I knew – you know already.

My son took me into emergency, through a thick fog. This was a surprise, as it was mid-summer and Melbourne is not a polluted city. In fact, we don't have polluted cities in Australia. This was not really a fog. It was smoke which had blown more than a thousand kilometres, from the bushfires which were raging in Northern New South Wales. We expect beautiful blue skies in summer. So this was a bit alarming.

I spent the day in the hospital having tests and watching the TV news as the story of the fires unfolded. Scott Morrison (the Prime Minister) had just received a lot of flak for taking his family to Hawaii, during a national emergency. So he rushed back to Australia to do a walkabout tour of the fires with his wife, in an effort to redeem himself. Unfortunately, the local MP had been fire-fighting all night and day – and the Prime Minister got himself sworn at and asked to get out of the way.

Another news story – A young cattle farmer (with a curly black beard) was shown on camera, begging the Prime Minister to save his herd of cattle from being roasted alive.

No help was at hand.  The loss of cattle was devastating to the live-stock industry.  And to billions of wild animals, too.

*Australia's bushfire crisis was one of the worst wildlife disasters in modern history. The fires killed or displaced nearly 3 billion animals.*

*Uprooting families and claiming lives, bushfires raged across Australia from June 2019 to February 2020. New WWF research reveals that the toll on wildlife was around three times higher than an earlier study estimated.*

*In total, 143 million mammals, 2.46 billion reptiles, 180 million birds, and 51 million frogs were harmed. "It's a difficult number to comprehend," said Professor Chris Dickman of the University of Sydney.*

Getting back to my health problem, the hospital doctor (a kindly Indian lady) diagnosed an inner ear problem.  She explained that my balancing mechanism in my ear has become a bit faulty. Sudden movements can confuse it. It took emergency action, and made me throw myself in the opposite direction.

"If you feel yourself losing balance, sit down immediately. Wherever you may be. Before you start throwing yourself around," said she. And she prescribed me some sea-sickness tablets, to carry with me always.

Good advice. So far, I haven't had any more bad experiences. But it does explain how I broke my wrists. On both occasions, I threw myself through the air, backwards.

## Disaster in Wuhan

A few weeks later, the first signs of the now infamous Pandemic, were reported from Wuhan in China. Twitter was showing sketches of health workers in full PPE, zipping struggling patients into body bags. Wuhan is an industrial hub, and heavily populated. Now trains were passing through without stopping. Their mayor was in tears on TV, people were dropping dead in the streets. The airport was closed. Australian citizens, who had gone home to Wuhan to celebrate the Chinese New Year with their loved ones, found themselves stranded. Our PM was begging the New Zealand PM to help get Australian citizens out of Wuhan and back home.

I was horrified. Was Scott Morrison trying to kill us all? First the fires (still raging) and now the plague? This was a "zoonotic" virus, that is a virus that has jumped from another species and is consequently, incredibly dangerous to humans. Not at all the same as rescuing people from a tsunami.

Everyone who didn't follow the news was quite unconscious of the situation. And a lot of people were not watching the news, because the bushfires had been so upsetting. Channel 9 was the only channel covering the story. After a deal was made to open Wuhan airport for a Qantas plane to pick up the Australian Chinese stranded there, Channel 9 sent a reporter to film the arrivals, who were all wearing black facemasks. It was a late-night flight and no sign of officialdom at the airport.

A passenger said into the microphone, "Wake up Australia!"

It took some time for Australia to wake up to the situation. After the Pandemic was declared, ABC got into covering the Pandemic all the time, which was a bit too much really.

Bringing the Chinese home did not result in an outbreak, I am glad to say. With their experience of SARS, most of them were very careful, and not many were infected. One man did report to his GP, saying that he thought he had the virus, but the doctor didn't know anything about it. So he took himself to emergency. Another had a birthday party in a Chinese restaurant, and someone at another table got sick, but there was no spread of deadly infection. 9 News was raising questions about allowing thousands of Chinese students to come back to Australia, for the new academic year.

I was getting really upset. The news coming from Wuhan was dubbed Fake News. Dreadful things were happening overseas, but our government wasn't even in session. It seems that most of our cabinet was in Washington, having economics related discussions with the US pollies. Ironically, our Minister for Border Control, Peter Dutton, returned home from the US, with the infection. He had to go into home isolation. So did the PM (as a primary contact), whilst vehemently declaring he would never miss out on supporting his football team! Which, of course, he had to.

To offset my anxiety, which made me curl up under my bedsheets, I tried writing letters to MPs, the PM, the newspapers etc, suggesting that people entering Australia should go into quarantine, and overseas students should remain in their own country and study on line. Not a great change, as they were already working online most of the time. The Age published my letter on 31st January, together with a letter from a school principal complaining that she could not find out which of her students had recently returned from China, as that information was with the Federal government and so unavailable to the Victorian Education Dept. The PM sent an automated out-of-office reply. So did Mr Dutton's office.

A friend in Malaysia had sent me a link to an English language South China News website, showing a huge, prefabricated hospital being built for corona virus patients. The time-frame for the job was 7 days. Imagine trying to do that in Australia! It would take at least 2 years to get planning permission. Indeed, it took nearly a year for the government to send prefabs to the fire-and-flood stricken citizens of Mallacoota, in Victoria.

What I am trying to tell you is, that I peaked early on with having anxiety attacks about the pandemic. I was anxious before it even happened: before the World Health Organisation declared a Pandemic, and before the virus was named Covid-19. That is the downside of being a science teacher. We understand too much about what is happening to the planet. I was terrified that my darling grandchildren might succumb. As we now know, the danger was to the elderly. So far, little children have been resistant, but no-one knew that at the time.

I actually felt calmer when the situation came out into the open, and the danger was recognised. There were slight signs of government action, at last. But terrible things were happening at sea.

My friend Helen and I had booked a transit cruise to Hawaii, departing Sydney on March 24th 2020, and calling at Tonga and some other South Pacific islands. After the Australian summer, cruise ships in the South Pacific relocate to Alaska for the Northern summer. And vice versa after the Northern summer. Not being very keen on long flights, and wanting to see Hawaii, we had booked the cruise the year before (with a holiday in Hawaii and a return flight).

**March 6th**. Helen and I had taken out an "Any Reason" cancellation insurance on the Hawaii holiday, but not on the cruise. We used the insurance to cancel the US holiday on the 6th March. The cruise looked unlikely to go ahead, as the Pacific Islanders were closing their ports in self-defence. Then we received an email bribing us with onboard spending vouchers if we rebooked on a future cruise. Clearly the ship was not taking guests for the transit voyage. We let the cruise line cancel it. We did not lose our money, but it was touch-and-go with the timing.

It was ten months before the travel agent coughed up our refund!   The cruise line claimed that they had refunded immediately.

At that time, there was still a belief that ships not stopping in China would not be affected.  Of course that was not the case.  Passengers world-wide were flying in on Bucket List tours and landing and boarding in Australia without quarantine.  Crew members were transferring from one ship to another.  And people could be infectious with no symptoms at all.

**11th March 2020**, the Director General of the World Health Organisation declared

*"In the past two weeks, the number of cases of COVID-19 outside China has increased 13-fold, and the number of affected countries has tripled.*

*There are now more than 118,000 cases in 114 countries, and 4,291 people have lost their lives.*

*Thousands more are fighting for their lives in hospitals.*

*In the days and weeks ahead, we expect to see the number of cases, the number of deaths, and the number of affected countries climb even higher.*

*WHO has been assessing this outbreak around the clock and we are deeply concerned both by the alarming levels of*

*spread and severity, and by the alarming levels of inaction.*

*We have therefore made the assessment that COVID-19 can be characterized as a pandemic."*

Strange to say, our PM passed this information on to the nation with a Pandemic Cash Boost Bonanza speech. This referred to a one-off $750 payment to pensioners etc, but he did not authorise travellers to cancel. Consequently, holiday makers were setting off to the destinations that their travel agents had picked for them. Some may have weighed the odds on catching a fatal disease, but most were quite unaware. Consequently, some elderly and very sick tourists had to be rescued by Qantas on mercy missions.

**19th March 2020**. The Ruby Princess disembarked 2,700 passengers in Sydney harbour, after a trip to New Zealand. The night before, the ship had signalled the need for hospitalisation of a few passengers with acute respiratory symptoms, but the local Ambulance Service had refused on the grounds that they were not equipped to handle Covid. The ship was asked to stand off-shore and berth early in the morning, so that sick passengers could be tested for Covid and influenza. They were tested, but due to "inadequate protocols" for infectious diseases, all the passengers were hastily disembarked before receiving the results.

Just now, I looked up "protocol" in several sources, including Wiki, and couldn't find anything to match the use above. As far as I can make out, "protocol" is being used to describe a list of actions to be taken by administrators, who have never been trained to think, or allowed to make any decisions of their own. Protocols are most probably written by lawyers, so would be quite inexplicable anyway!

Neither the crew nor the passengers were aware of the situation. It turned out that at least 576 passengers tested positive for Covid-19. Some went home to retirement villages, and some flew back to their home countries, so the whole thing was a worry. But as the Premier of New South Wales pointed out at the time, "We are still having thousands of people coming in on planes, every day."

That was the start of the whole Pandemic thing. Since then we have had lockdowns, leaks from hotel quarantine, school closures, vaccinations and frustrations. But at least we haven't suffered the disasters that have befallen many other countries in the world. To date (July 2022) there have been around 8,000 Covid-19 deaths altogether in Australia – compared with 185,000 in the UK and more than a million in the USA. So we can count ourselves lucky.

I am sitting at my kitchen table, researching this chapter, and getting fearful because I am booked to go with friends on a Pacific cruise in Quantum of the Seas, coming up in November 2022 (3 months' time). I had Covid last month, and I had already had two booster injections. But I just read that immunity cannot be guaranteed. I could get reinfected, right now.

# **Lament of the Over Seventy**

Maybe,

Covid was invented

By a sadist, ageist

Spoilsport

To stop us living more than

Our three-score-and ten.

Was it really so wrong

To have fun and live long?

I was feeling healthy

And getting a bit wealthy

But now we no longer belong.

Cruising's a disaster

And may never survive after.

It must find another clientele.

Else every Princess

Like the Marie Celeste

Will float like a ghost on the swell.

The U3A

Is a very nice way

To share skills and challenge my brain.

We can do something online

Which may be quite fine
But I wonder if we'll meet again.

If you're still feeling young
And springily-sprung
You can go for a walk
But stand back if you talk
To the people you meet on the way.

So is Covid a clock
Which goes tick-tock
Or just that some oldies are weak?
Can we be allowed
To meet in a crowd?
Or is our time up, so to speak.

The experts say
The virus will still stay
After the pandemic goes away.
It may always be there
To catch us unaware...
It could come back any day.

So what can we do
To see this through

And go back to the life that we knew?

Will we ever?

Maybe never.

Sadly, that could be true

# Cruise-ships Galore and no tourism? (Winter 2020)

*These are the thoughts I had at the time.   Hopefully that time is past.   Cruising is now back on track and cruising fans are getting right into it and making up for lost time.*

A long time ago in the 60s, I was stuck in Cairo for a few days with nothing to do. I saw a ship at anchor, at the end of a very long gangplank, so I walked down it. There was a receptionist sitting at a small table.

"Excuse me," said I, "Do you go to Alexandria?"

"No, Madam ," he replied haughtily, "this is the Nile Hilton ."

It just occurred to me, that the same fate could be the solution for all the empty cruise ships lying at anchor around the oceans of the world.

After all, a cruise is the ultimate holiday. There is no real need to bump about on the sea. You can go on excursions ashore, just like you do on real cruises. I'm serious, just think about it.  You can stay in and go to the theatre, go to a bar, go dancing or fling yourself down a waterslide and enjoy unlimited food and entertainment. All without getting off the ship. Plus you don't have to mingle with the local inhabitants on the streets unless you want to – but if you do want to go ashore, you don't have to be back on the boat by 5pm and then rush off to the next place. Great for a weekend or a full-blown holiday. The only problem is that the ships have to go to sea regularly to repower, and they are probably a bit too large for coastal trips. They might start bashing into each other.

But the great thing about this is: the Australian dollar stays at home. It doesn't just leak straight out of the economy. (I might be being a bit fanciful there. The shipping companies will find a way to keep it!)

Apart from my little idea, what about the future of Australian domestic tourism? Firstly, there is a lot of preparation to be done. When I mention to people that Australia is an amazing country for holidaying and so why are travel agents bundling everyone off far off, foreign places - there is cry of "Holidays in Australia are so expensive." They don't have to be. Lots of people are letting out units via Airbnb or Booking.com etc. With enough people travelling, group travel is possible, by air, coach or train. It just needs organising. And facilitating. With more demand, there can be more flights and trains.

What I am trying to say is, that it quite possible to make tourism accessible in Australia. The Chinese found it accessible. And they come from a long way away. I took a boat trip out to the reef at Cairns, with 250 Chinese and only half a dozen people who weren't Chinese. The Asians were very well regimented in the care of their own trainers and swimming instructors. Hardly any of the Asian tourists could swim. Which meant that, at the outer reef, I had to cope with a crowd of people holding on to ship's life belts together. Never again. I saw no fish.

One of my most spectacular holidays ever, was hiring a sailing-boat with friends and sailing around the Whitsunday Islands, stopping at coves you can reach no other way. I can highly recommend it. Sheltered water within the Great Barrier reef, and no master's ticket required!

# STRUGGLING WITH TECHNOLOGY

## Parking Limbo

My friend Christine is having a surgical procedure at the Royal Women's hospital in Melbourne, and I promised to be with her before. Only I have a problem. I decided to drive to the hospital in my husband's keyless Lexus, because it has a SATNAV, and my Honda doesn't. He is overseas, so not using it. And now I am stuck.

I have found street parking next to the hospital, and was reversing into it, when the car stopped moving. I think it has stalled, but I am not sure, because it is a hybrid and might just be silently resting. The rear-end is in, but the front is overlapping another car. To make things more panicky, the steering has locked.

I am pretty sure there is nothing wrong with the car. There is a procedure for starting a keyless car and I am not sure if am doing it right. I mean, I managed to start it when I left home, but I may have forgotten something. At any rate, the accelerator is not responding. I just need someone to tell me what to do. I try phoning a friend with a Lexus, but she hasn't the faintest. I try ringing my sons, but they are not answering.

I phone the RACV. Do I have my membership number? No. I explain that I am driving a new Lexus and I can't make it move. Oh, then you need Lexus Assist, not the RACV. They will come out to you.

Just then, there is a tap on the window. A Vietnamese gentleman is trying to attract my attention. I roll down the window.

*"Excuse me," says he, "If you are not using this parking space, would you mind moving out of it?"*

*"I'm trying, but it won't start."*

*"Obviously, the ignition key is missing!"*

*"It doesn't have one!"*

*"Well, hadn't you better find it?"*

Having got rid of him, I phone Christine and tell her I am having problem parking. She says OK, she thinks she will be a while yet.

Next, I try phoning Lexus Brighton. They put me on hold. Now I am really worried because my phone battery is running out. I didn't think to bring an iPhone cord with me. Another tap on the window.

This time it is an elderly Scot.

*"Excuse me, would you have a wrench in your toolkit?"*

*"Sorry, I am on a call."*

I am really frustrated.  At last, I get through to the service department and they don't help me. They tell me to phone Lexus Assist.  I ask for the number, and they haven't got it. They say it's on a card in the glove box.  I look but it's not there.

Now I'm shouting, rather rudely I am ashamed to say.

*"I have been stuck here for half-an-hour and the number should be painted in large red numbers on the windscreen!"*

Another tap on the window:

*"You wouldna be telling me that a brand-new Lexus has nae a toolkit in the boot?  I canna get the steering-lock off my wheel."*

It is a well-known fact, that the people who lock up their cars with a portable steering lock, own cars that nobody could possibly want to steal. Not even for a joyride. Come to think of it, especially not for a joyride. But I decide to help him, and we take a look in the boot. Sure enough, there is a great big toolkit in a compartment under the spare. He takes what he wants and returns it.

At this point, my son William rings me back. I explain what happened in detail.

*"Give the steering wheel a tug, Mum."*

*"It doesn't move."*

*"Pull harder Mum. YOU CAN'T HURT IT!"*

He is right. Problem solved.

Parked at last. And Christine hasn't gone into theatre yet. I have brought her a book I know she will enjoy – The No.1 Ladies Detective Agency by Alexander McCall Smith.

All's well that ends well.

# That Mykie thing!

## 2014

*"I forgot about this Mykie thing"*

*"What did you forget about it?" asked the railway officer.*

*"All of it. I don't often take the train"*

I'm getting agitated because I am on my way to the Writers' Festival, and I forgot that you can no longer buy a train ticket at the station. In fact, I forgot my Mykie even existed. When I was leaving the house, I grabbed some things out of my handbag, and stuffed them in my briefcase – no need to carry two bags! Actually, it's not a briefcase, it's a big pink beach-bag which doubles as my computer bag. It's light, flat and very handy. It was an instant decision to travel light, when I realised that my first event was right by the station, and so decided to go by train. I chucked in my "Events" tickets, some paper money, a notebook, a pen and a crossword puzzle book. (I'm hooked on cryptics at the moment). And I chucked out my computer and  my heavy wallet (brim full of credit cards). So I thought I was organised, but I forgot all about my Mykie.

Mykie is not new, it's been around for a few years. The first year doesn't really count, because the system was full of bugs. So there were still ticket machines. But now, Mykie is the only way. You carry a ticket which you can charge up. That's fine for regular travellers, but a real pain it you hardly ever indulge in public transport. The thing is, you can't just rock up at the station and grab a ticket and jump on the train. Well you can, if it's a big station that has the right machine to issue a new card. And even if there is one, you still have to figure out which buttons you have to press. Now I do have a bit of tech savvy. After all, I'm in software development. But when I'm faced with a machine with a lot of buttons and meaningless hieroglyphics I am inclined to panic.

You see, I haven't travelled by train for yonks. I hate travelling by public transport. It involves a lot of walking, and standing on station platforms in intense heat, icy rain, or a howling gale (this is Melbourne we are talking about), and doing far more exercise than I feel good about.

I mean this is my track record on travelling by train – in the once or twice a year that I do it:

(1) Taking my granddaughter Billie to the zoo. My daughter announced that we would be much faster on the train and insisted on dropping us at Batman station. Yes, it really is called Batman, named after John Batman, an early Australian colonialist and adventurer (nothing to do with the movies). But neither Batman nor the zoo station, had a Mykie dispensing machine, so we had to travel illegally both ways. I felt awfully nervy about breaking the law with a toddler in a pusher. Would that be seriously irresponsible grand-parenting?

(2) Train derailed at Seaford. I don't know what's wrong with Seaford, but it has more than its share of derailments. Not serious but very inconvenient. It's only two stops from the end of the line, so they can run a bus. I tried the bus ride once. It took forever to turn up, and we were all treated to a shouted conversation (from back to front of the bus) between a male and female passenger who had somehow discovered that they had a job in common – culling kangaroos with a rifle and with or without a helicopter. A gruesome conversation which I did not enjoy.

(3) Trying to travel to the Melbourne Film Festival on a Sunday, checking the departure times and deciding it would be quicker to get back into the car and take the freeway (not much traffic on Sunday).

(4) Lots of minor catastrophes and delays, including "railway lines warped by heatwave".

So as you can see, every journey puts me off for another year. Another reason I was freaked about forgetting the existence of Mykie, was that (being 11am) all the free places in the station car park were taken up by commuters. So I had to park in the next car park which is five dollars to park all day. Not a bad price, but when I drew a five dollar note out of my pink bag, I couldn't find a slot to put it in! This machine only takes coins. No plastic either. And I hadn't put any coins in my coat packet. Oh, what a relief, I've got change in the car! But is it enough for a Mykie card as well?

The thing about Mykie is, that it's almost perfect for a regular traveller. But if you go to the city once a year, like me, then odds are that you can't remember where you put it. Or even that it exists!

## Lost key panic!

2012

I had a bit of a panic on Saturday morning. The plan was that Heidi and family were dropping in for a social visit and to pick up their dog (they'd been on a camping holiday in a nature reserve so Tjillyi couldn't go with them).

The trouble started when Heidi phoned and said, "Change of plan, you're coming here for Brunch and then we are taking the dogs to the beach." Heidi, Andy and Billie were staying at her in-laws in Mt Martha (not far off) because Grandad Jo had just come out of hospital.

So I rushed around and changed into beach clothes, put the dog in the car (my little gold keyless Lexus) and what did it tell me? "Key not detected".

My handbag was in the car. So why wasn't the key in it? What did I do yesterday? Whatever was I wearing?

Then I remembered that I completely emptied my handbag out in the back of my friend Christine's car the night before, by accident when I was looking for my house keys. We were having a girls' night out, to an orchestral concert in Melbourne.    I did find the coffee beans (essential for keeping awake during the performance) on the seat, but as the "keyless" key is black plastic with no metal parts, it would have been very hard to see on black leather, and so I could have overlooked it.

But there was a problem. I phoned Christine and she was  going to Sydney for the week-end and already at the airport. Therefore, not possible to check if I left them in her car.

It was doubly frustrating, because I was driving up to Melbourne for a 50th Wedding anniversary, at lunchtime.

So I started desperately looking for my spare key. Which I hadn't seen for ages. I knew I put it away in a safe place, because if I inadvertently have two keys in the car, I have to find both of them before it will let me lock it up and leave it!

I know you are now thinking I'm going gaga!  No, I'm not, but I admit I can't keep track of all these small objects. Modern tech has gone too far. It's getting worse and worse. Who designs all this rubbish anyway? If you are going to make car keys so complicated, then at least have a system for finding them. I mean, something you can switch on which is screwed to the wall, and will immediately tell you where the key is. That might work.

So I started on the quest of finding my spare car keys by letting the car find them. First, I threw all my handbags into the car. Still not detected. Then I threw all my coats into the car. Still no result. Then my trousers. No good.

Then I tried to phone Heidi, but she was a having a technological misunderstanding with her mobile, so I had to phone the land-line. Nana Jan answered and she was in a panic. Grandad Jo was in the garden with a gun, threatening to shoot ducks. He had bought some large plastic swans to frighten the ducks off the pool (algae love duck poo) and that worked for a while. The plastic swans are white, which is all wrong for Australia (our swans are black all over) and that seemed enough to scare any Australian duck, but now they seem to have got used to them.

I said, "If it was my husband' I would shoot him,' and Jan said, 'You can come over and shoot mine!" which is probably why Heidi and Co immediately decided to go back to plan A and come to my place for brunch.

By the time they arrived, I had found a spare key which I had completely forgotten was a key. It looks like a rather thick credit card. I stopped using it shortly after getting the car, because it fell out of my wallet whenever I used money. Panic over, but still a right-mess from all the cupboards and drawers I turned out.

The week-end went to plan after that.

On Monday, I found the missing key in the laundry basket. In the pocket of my jeans. I must have taken them off, when I changed into my shorts to go to the beach!

# NBN AND SMART PHONES

My telephone exchange was one of the first to succumb to the NBN rollout– the National Broadband Network. Farewell to the telephone exchange! Say hallo to the internet.

Five years later, the rollout is still going on, and causing an enormous amount of confusion. It is made more confusing by the fact that there are different versions of it. In my version, two little Indian guys with spades, had to dig a trench all the way to my front door (all government initiatives seem to involve imported Indian labour}. Our house is behind the next-door neighbours', so the driveway is more than a hundred metres long. When they finally reached the house, they put a box of electronics on the outside wall. A few weeks later, a local electrician came and connected the box to another box and a modem, inside the house. He explained that my landline would soon cease to work. No-one else had mentioned that and I didn't quite take it in.

About mid-day on Sunday, his prophecy came true. My phone stopped working. I went down to the Telstra shop, and they said 'Yes, you've been disconnected from the

Exchange, you are on NBN now." So I tried to buy one of their phones, but guess what, they didn't sell NBN phones. They sent me to JB Hifi. Now you would think that, as Telstra is a major player in the telephone and internet industry, they would stock the relevant phone, wouldn't you? Anyway, no big deal. I bought a phone with 3 handsets for $99.

## Don't phone me on my home-phone!

Please don't phone me on my home-phone because I can't find it. You would think that having 3 handsets would help, but it works the other way round. There are 3 charging stands for the handsets, each one on a short power lead. The ringing comes from the master hub by the modem, which is no help finding the handsets. Unfortunately, all my power points are under furniture.

If I am lucky, I do find a handset but of course, the battery is flat. By the time I find another handset, the phone has stopped ringing. If it is charged, I look up the missed call, but if you put the phone down just after I pick up mine – then I have no way of finding you. As I very rarely use the home phone, the batteries are unlikely to be charged.

## Getting back to the NBN thing

The internet worked well but I had problems with the phone connection. So I phoned the help-line (from my mobile) and got connected to a Telstra support guy in the Philippines. He said I would soon be connected. I thought I'd check a few things, and this is how the conversation went:

*Me:  Can you tell me how much it will cost to a make a call to England, on my new contract?*

*Him:  Where exactly?*

*Me (a bit surprised): Either London or Newcastle-upon-Tyne.*

*Him:  Can you hold a minute?*

*After five minutes of holding music,*

*Him: I've found England, it's in the UK!*

*Now if only I had thought to tell him that.  As an English woman, I felt a bit sad to think that England had lost its place in the world.*

A few days later, the phone was still not working, so I phoned the support line again.  This time, I spoke with a girl who was more sophisticated.  While she was waiting, she chatted along nicely.

*Her: Are you ready for Thanksgiving?*

*Me: No, we don't do Thanksgiving here.*

*Her: How come?*

*Me: I'm in Australia.*

*Her, puzzled: I thought you did Thanksgiving everywhere in America.*

In all fairness, I think that management should put a World Map on the wall, to show their staff which country they are servicing.

At least I had NBN (even if it wasn't switched on) when my phone stopped working. I know people who tried to ignore NBN altogether, and ended up with no phone at all. Someone I know, who has steadfastly resisted technology and does not have a mobile phone or Wi-fi, was upset and astonished to receive a letter saying that her phone was about to be cut off, because the exchange was closing down. She said her boyfriend asked the neighbours and found that everyone else had connected to NBN.

*Me: You need to get a mobile.*

*Her, indignantly: I don't need one. I listen to my messages when I get home, and phone back when I have time for a chat.*

Times have changed and not everyone has changed with them. Once upon a time, when a penny was a lot of money, people made a penny phone call and had a good, long talk. Then phoning started being timed by the minute and became very expensive. That was back in the 1960s. Since then, there has been a whole history of changes. Young people abandoned the landline, because line rental was so expensive and not needed with a mobile. Mobile phones came into their own at the turn of the century, but the smart phone has now changed everything. It has turned into the most user-friendly computer ever.

Now, we use the phone to find each other, or make a quick arrangement to meet. It is incredibly convenient. A wonderful tool. But many senior citizens are technophobic. Smart phones are too much of a challenge. For a person who has never used a computer, it is all too hard. How can you order an Uber or taxi without the App? How can you do banking when the banks are closing down their branches? We are getting to the stage when nothing can be done without the internet, and this is very unfair on senior citizens.

## The University of the Third Age

I am a volunteer tutor at the U3A (the University of the 3rd age). It is a world-wide organisation, for retired people to share their skills with other senior citizens, and for everyone to socialise a bit. I find that not many of my class members have access to streaming documentaries at home. At the time of writing, Netflix is enormously popular, and quite cheap, but you do need a smart TV, or a casting gadget and a smart phone (or tablet). Anytime free-to-air television is coming into its own, but there again, the same problem. All this is unknown territory for many seniors. I tried giving out a list of docos to watch during a Covid-19 lockdown, but no takers. Unless the docos are free to air on ABC (which is definitely their most popular TV channel) they won't watch them at home.

Once upon a time, phoning was simple. We knew exactly where to find the phone – it was wired to the wall. We didn't have to choose one, unless we really wanted to. But now, there are too many choices, all competing against each other. I googled "Seniors packages" to see if there were any good deals tailored to seniors. There were quite a few advertisers, but when I phoned the numbers, the sales people had no idea how to start the conversation, or what was being advertised.

For a mobile, we can have an iPhone or Galaxy or whatever, and this is just the brand name of the phone. Not to be confused with the name of the service provider. For that we can choose between Vodaphone, Telstra, Optus or half-a-dozen other companies. This is all very hard to understand. Completely confusing.

There are a whole range of choices on how you buy your phone time, how much data you want to download, how fast and so on. Plus the same sort of options for your NBN services - what speed, how many bytes, do you want wi-fi, do you need a home phone. As far as the uninitiated are concerned, it might as well be rocket science.

In short, a complete overload of inexplicable information.

# Oh my gov!

2021

I have been watching a Logie winning Australian office-sitcom called UTOPIA. It's a tongue-in-cheek story which comes all too close to reality. Set in the Nation Building Authority (NBA) offices, which is a fictional government department, we follow the working lives of the characters therein. Each episode features a Federal Government initiative, which never gets off the ground. There have been four series, starting in 2014. It is all too familiar, as there are real events (or should I say non-events, because this is a tale of frustration) which are quite recognisable. It is a very drole lesson on how government operates (or fails to operate). I can truly say that I have endured and survived these government mishaps. The Mygov website, for example.

*Episode 19, 2017, Nation Shapers: This episode features an IT project (mygov.com.au) which has consistently failed and is handed over to our fictitious NBA guys to put right. Two young programmers give a presentation to Nat, before handing it over.*

*Nat tries unsuccessfully to sign in, which puzzles the programmers who quickly type in some code, which does the trick. (Moral, programmers should not be allowed to check their own work. They don't know that, unlike the potential user, they are typing code). At that point, all her contacts disappear from her smart phone.*

# A nice, warm fuzzy feeling

Now, I'll tell you my version of the Mygov story. Please notice the name - mygov.com.au. "My" gives the name "inclusivity" (so important nowadays, according to the spin doctors) and links it to government (to tell us that they are looking after us). We should all have a nice, warm, fuzzy feeling when we try desperately to get our Child Allowance, or a Pension or go into Age-care.

I decided to retire (long overdue) and go on the pension. I was told that I should apply online on Mygov. There, I had to download about 20 forms and answer ridiculous questions such as:

*"In the last five years, have you (or your partner) given away, or sold for less than their market value, or surrendered a right to any cash, assets, property or income?"*

I am not joking, that is a real question. It even asks for details: date sold, amount paid etc. I can't make out whether that would be a negative or a positive on the pension calculation.

I will give you a few examples of what went wrong. This is an abridged version. It took me more than two years to get my pension, and one more year to get more than a miniscule amount. Lucky I wasn't sleeping on a park bench!

First, I was told I was not eligible for a pension for another year, because I had just been paid a year's pay in advance. This was because I was being paid through a family trust, but I had been paid monthly, as a salary. Apparently, the company accounts did not show that.

According to the government, beneficiary payments are in advance. Which is just weird. I was determined to ensure that I was eligible for a pension, so I waited a year and lived on my savings, but there was more trouble to come, when I tried to use the website.

These are just highlights.

1. At some time in the past, the sign in had been to "Centrelink". Every time I signed in, it bounced me back and forth between Mygov and Centrelink and demanded different passwords.

2. I tried saying I had forgotten my password, but that was even more disastrous.

3. It changed the date we bought the house, to the date we took out citizenship, and would not let me correct it.

4. My house is on two titles, because it has a granny flat, which threw the program entirely. It did a bit of computer think and came up with a whole lot of questions about farm buildings and what business we were doing in the farm and so on, and I could not get out of this cycle.

5.  Every now and then, a screen would pop up saying that I needed to choose a link (none of which worked) and sign on with my new Mygov code. As I had never had another code, this didn't make sense.

    Much later, when I was desperate to sort the mess out and get some money out of the government, I realised that the screen came up when I took too long to figure out the answer to a question. It was supposed to be the time-out screen, but because that screen had the same URL indexing as an old screen, and I hadn't cleared my browser, it threw me back in time to an old version of the website. I apologise if this is all gobbledy-gook to you, but it was pretty gobbledy-gook to me too. The thing is, I gave up, and if I hadn't given up, I would have known that the website had put in a fictitious salary of forty-eight thousand a year. Which reduced my pension to almost nothing.

6.  It asked for contact details but rejected my email address. My email address was compulsorily my ID , so I didn't worry too much. This turned out to be a serious mistake.

7.  The Health Card. I could have had it while I was working and saved a lot on prescriptions. About 9 months after achieving my pension, I went to the chemist and found that my Health Card had been stopped. I then realised that my microscopic pension wasn't coming in either. This spurred me on to try and get something done. I tracked down a helpful person on the telephone:

    *She: You failed to reply to a message on your Mygov.*

*Me: I didn't know I had to watch it.*

*She: We couldn't email you because you didn't fill in your email address.*

*Me: The ID is the email address. You must have that.*

*She: You need to go into Mygov and read the email.*

*Me: What does it say?*

*She: You must apply for a UK pension.*

*Me: That's OK, I've started getting one.*

*She: We have to subtract your UK pension from your Australian pension.*

A word about my UK pension. It is not income-tested. It depends on how many health stamps your employers have paid, over your working years. When I first signed on for the pension, I had the choice to delay it, as it is taxable income. So I did, and I was quite excited when I received a payment of $130 in my bank account. I wondered if it was a weekly payment. I was very disappointed to find that it was an annual one. Like a sort of marker to say that I was listed as a pensioner. Later on, I actually received a lump sum when I did retire, which helped me survive what was going on with my Australian pension.

I had to call the UK Pensions office in Newcastle-upon-Tyne, to find out what I was eligible for. A nice lady answered me.

*Me: Who was the last employer to pay my stamps?*

*She: I am not allowed to tell you that.*

*Me: Can you give me a clue?*

*She: Think of a fruit.*

*Me: Really? A fruit?*

*She: Your address.*

*Me: Oh! Do you mean Strawberry Hill?*

We were living in Strawberry Hill, on a boat on the river Thames. I was teaching part-time at Thames Valley Grammar. It was very nice of them to pay my stamps. All the other schools, in the seven years that I taught part-time with a growing family, didn't bother. Apparently, they were not obliged to. I didn't know.

## You have been chosen

December 2020, I received an email from Mygov, instructing me that I had been chosen to submit an updated profile by December 19th. This involved filling in a 19-page Centrelink form, plus submitting proofs of identity and citizenship etc. I had scheduled this time for my Christmas cards and letters. There were threats of imprisonment if I answered anything incorrectly. I was completely freaked out. I needed my accountant and my stockbroker to make sense of the questions.

Fortunately, both were available. Unfortunately, after uploading all 26 pages to Mygov, when I pressed Submit, it spat them out again. This happened repeatedly. This was happening to everybody, because the form was not listed in the choices for upload.

I was told to post it. Another dilemma! I had filled the form in pencil, and I had to ink over all my answers.

# Change of Circumstances

As luck would have it, when I decided to take up a consultancy job and get away from the pension, Mygov had just been through another overhaul. I must report my "change of circumstances" within a fortnight or I will find myself in big trouble.

Like many websites today, the intention of the new "self-serve" Mygov is to stop anybody from having to answer the telephone. Theoretically, you can do it all yourself. That is, you can find the form you need and download it. But there doesn't seem to be any way of inputting info about myself. None of the forms are relevant. There are some telephone numbers, but when I ring, a robot tells me to go to the website. After messing about with telephone menus for a few hours, I get put through to Reporting a Change of Circumstance. A robotic voice said, "You are not registered for reporting, bye-bye".

# Technophobia or Dementia?

Finally, I find a section on the Mygov Website for helping Aged Australians. The implication being that only extreme technophobia or dementia, could prevent me from going self-service.

After being on hold for an hour, I do get through to a real person, and accidentally cut myself off whilst looking up some personal info on my phone. I am hoping that she will ring me back – but no. I go on hold again. Another lady answers, and tells me that unfortunately, they are not allowed to ring out. Anyway, she does register me for "reporting income". After that, all plain sailing, hopefully.

It was at this point that a made a fatal mistake. I accepted the invitation to make Mygov easier by downloading the App. Click here to Download. I did. After all, I was logged in on a government website. The next screen told me to download my free Driver. A bit strange, but I obeyed. The next screen told me I had 14 out-of-date drivers and asked for $47 for a driver service. That was very suss and I closed the screen but failed to power-off the computer. The suss screen kept coming up, while I was working. Until my computer switched off altogether and would not start up at all. What a dilemma!

I finished this book on my new computer.

# EPILOGUE

## Australia the Beautiful

After weeks of rain, the sky is a perfect sky-blue. On a day like today, I can't believe how lucky I am! I am sitting at the breakfast table, looking out through the patio window at the spring flowers in full bloom around the pool. The pool fence is completely obscured by bright red bottlebrushes, purple native hibiscus and pink pelargoniums. A noisy miner bird is very busy, gathering nectar from the bottlebrush blooms, tearing the petals as he pecks into them. Fortunately, there are hundreds of blooms, and even more on a pink bottlebrush, which is now in bud. The honey-eaters' job is to pollinate flowers, as they stuff themselves with high-energy nectar. An essential service. The birds and the bees.

Australian magpies (so called because they are black and white) are pulling worms out of the ground and singing beautiful songs. A kookaburra is perched in a small gumtree, his blue wing coverts sparkling in the sunshine. He sits perfectly still, listening for earthworms near the surface of the lawn.  Suddenly he swoops, and plucks out a fat earthworm for his breakfast.

I feel like I am living in a bird park!  Even better, these birds are completely wild and visiting of their own free will. Unafraid of humans but territorial toward other birds. It is as if they are living in a parallel universe, and we don't matter, unless we mess it up.

The widespread, leafless branches of a very tall, dead gumtree beyond the pool, make a wonderful perch for surveying the world. Suddenly, I see some small, green parrots flying toward it.  When they perch,  I see they are rainbow lorikeets and Eastern rosellas.   Rosellas, lorikeets and magpies are sitting in family groups, looking around and planning their day.

Australian birds are so colourful.  I love to sketch them.

This is a beautiful country.

Dear Reader,

Many thanks for reading my story. It is all quite true, as I remember. I hope you found it fun and interesting. If so, it would help tremendously if you would write a little review, telling other people what you enjoyed about it. So that they can enjoy it too. You can easily put your review under "Review this product" on the Amazon kindle page for my book. Or wherever you like. Without reviews, books can sink without trace.

Wishing you joy in life and good reads,

Mary Sanghvi

Printed in Great Britain
by Amazon